DERIVATIVES

A Manager's Guide to the World's Most Powerful Financial Instruments

PHILIP McBRIDE JOHNSON

McGraw-Hill

New York San Francisco Washington, D.C. Auckland Bogotá
Caracas Lisbon London Madrid Mexico City Milan
Montreal New Delhi San Juan Singapore
Sydney Tokyo Toronto

658.152
J68d

Library of Congress Cataloging-in-Publication Data

Johnson, Philip McBride.
    Derivatives : a managers guide to the world's most powerful
financial instruments / by Philip McBride Johnson.
      p. cm.
    ISBN 0-07-134506-X
    1. Derivatives securities.   I. Title.
  HG6024.A3J638   1999
  658.15'2--dc21   98-49918
                                      CIP

McGraw-Hill

A Division of The McGraw·Hill Companies

1 2 3 4 5 6 7 8 9 0 DOC/DOC 9 0 3 2 1 0 9 8

ISBN 0-07-134506-X

The sponsoring editor for this book was *Stephen Isaacs*, the editing supervisor was *John M.
Morriss*, and the production supervisor was *Suzanne W. B. Rapcavage*. It was set in 11/13
Palatino by Carlisle Communications, LTD.

McGraw-Hill books are available at special quantity discounts to use as premiums and
sales promotions, or for use in corporate training programs. For more information, please
write to the Director of Special Sales, McGraw-Hill, 11 West 19th Street, New York, NY
10011. Or contact your local bookstore.

This book is printed on recycled, acid-free paper containing a minimum of 50%
recycled de-inked fiber.

To all of the executives, at all levels on the organizational chart, who have confided to me or to other confidants their sheer terror at the prospect of losing sleep, their sanity, or—worst—their job because some derivatives "cowboy" beneath them in the chain of responsibility could blow up the company at any moment.

And to the derivatives trader who, I hope, will find it more difficult to do just that because the boss is a little better prepared thanks to this book.

CONTENTS

WHY BOTHER WITH THIS BOOK?   ix
INTRODUCTION   xi

Chapter 1

What Are Derivatives?   1

Futures Contracts   3
Options   6
Swaps   10
Hybrid Instruments   16
Forward Contracts   19
What Do You Mean "Commodity"?   20

Chapter 2

Why Do They Exist?   23

The Hedging Instinct   24
Honoring the "Speculator"   29

Chapter 3

Call in the Lawyers   31

Exchange-Traded Derivatives   32
Swap Agreements   35
Hybrid Instruments   37
Over-the-Counter Options   39
Forward Contracts   39
Playing the "Institutional" Card   41

Chapter 4

Where the Risks Are   43

Valuation Risk   43
Timing Risk   44

Credit Risk   46

Legal Risk   47

Operational Risk   48

Accounting Risk   50

Boundary Risk   52

Pollyanna Risk   54

"Forrest Gump" Risk   54

Pretty-Face Risk   55

Overharvesting Risk   56

Side-of-the-Angels Risk   57

Legal Double-Talk Risk   58

Ratings Risk   59

Career Risk   61

Chapter 5

A Case Study in Catastrophe—Sumitomo and the Copper Market   62

Background   62

Paying the Piper: The Massive CFTC Settlement   63

Chapter 6

The International Dimension   98

The Globalization Phenomenon   98

Cultural and Political Wild Cards   100

Coordinating Regulatory Policy   103

Chapter 7

Doing It Right   105

Living the Nightmare   105

Constructing a Good Plan   106

    Rule 1: Get Up to Speed   107

    Rule 2: The Selection Process   108

    Rule 3: Everyone Is a Company Player   109

    Rule 4: Information Is Power   110

    Rule 5: The Guillotine Effect   111

Chapter 8

What the Pros Recommend   113

Credit Risk   114
Liquidity Risk   117
Market Risk   118
Earnings Risk   119

Chapter 9

Preparing for the Future   121

The Rumored Demise of Open Outcry Trading   122
Deconstructing the Traditional Exchange   123
> *Step 1: Privatizing Exchange Ownership   125*
> *Step 2: Institutionalizing the Screen Dealing Mechanism   126*
> *Step 3: Operating the Self-Regulatory Program   126*
> *Step 4: The Clearing System   127*
> *Step 5: Liquidating Physical Assets   127*
> *Step 6: Forming the Trading Firm   128*
> *Step 7: The R&D Subsidiary   128*
Preparing for Regulatory Chaos   130

Chapter 10

The Political Dimension   132

The Agency Players   133
Congress   135
The States   137
The Media   139

CONCLUSION   140

Appendix A Report of the Board of Banking Supervision [Bank of England]
Inquiry in the Circumstances of the Collapse of Barings   141
Appendix B Excerpts from the *United States General Accounting Office Report on
Derivatives Losses Where Sales Abuses Were Alleged*   171

Appendix C Annex 1 through 6 to *Supervisory Information Framework for Derivatives and Trading Activities*—(Joint Report by the Basle Committee on Banking Supervision and the Technical Committee of the "IOSCO")   177

INDEX   205

Does it unnerve you a bit when people *think* they are explaining derivatives to you with the following:

$$P_6 = 1/\{[1 + F_1\,(D_1/360)] \times [1 + F_2\,(D_2/360)]\}$$

$$P_{12} = 1/\{[1 + F_1\,(D_1/360)] \times [1 + F_2\,(D_2/360)] \times [1 + F_3\,(D_3/360)] \times [1 + F_4\,(D_4/360)]\}$$

Do you believe that huge losses on derivatives are confined to reckless or dim-witted institutions? If so, consider:

Procter & Gamble (lost $102 million in 1994)

Gibson Greetings (lost $23 million in 1994)

Orange County, California (bankrupted after $1.7 *billion* loss in 1994)

Baring's Bank (bankrupted after $1.3 *billion* loss in 1995)

Sumitomo (lost $2.6 *billion* in 1996)

Government of Belgium ($1.2 *billion* loss in 1997)

National Westminster Bank (lost $143 million in 1997)

People who always fasten their seat belts, who replace the battery in their smoke alarms twice a year, and who recycle their trash may be taking a massive *job risk* by underestimating the danger of derivatives at their companies. This handbook is a painless way to learn the basics.

Philip McBride Johnson

This book is about the financial equivalent of fire. Wall Street engineers have constructed a vast array of new money instruments that, like fire, can do great good or wreak great devastation. The army of masters of business administration (finance) and other professionals, including not a few physicists, who conjure up these "financial products," cannot be expected to also perform other key functions like effective supervision and accurate risk management. Those duties fall mainly on you, the executive, and your staff. And, in the end, it is not only your organization's well-being that is at stake; *your career* also hangs in the balance!

Now that I have your attention, let me explain the purposes of this book. First, you should have a rudimentary understanding of the new "derivative" products, although scientific certainty is not required. In Chapter 1, I will introduce you to the several generic types of derivatives currently being offered and explain how each of them operates. In the process, you should gain a basic appreciation of why each of them has the potential to take your organization on a wild ride, or to actually make life less worrisome for it.

Considering the incendiary nature of these products, why are they even available? In Chapter 2, I will take you on a short journey through the evolution of derivatives, from the earliest standardized farm-oriented instruments to the current menagerie of products that may be hitched to anything from next season's hurricanes to pollution levels. In nearly every case, the designers have had as their objective to *reduce* business risks, usually by allowing organizations to hand off certain unwanted exposures to speculative daredevils who thrive on risk.

This is not a law book, and yet derivatives are not immune to legal risk. Various federal regulators are vying for the right to set standards and impose requirements on the sale and use of derivatives. Meanwhile, the architects and dealers of derivatives are resisting most efforts to impose any legal limits on their activities. In Chapter 3, you will learn a little about that legal skirmish so that, should you need to do so, you will know whether to call your lawyers.

The financial engineers create; they rarely monitor or supervise. At the same time, those who operate the trading desks for derivatives (which might include high-level treasury officers within your organization) are renowned for taking the short view: "What do you mean, 'the *long* run'?; in the long run we will all be dead!" And so the brunt of supervision and risk control must be borne by others, which may include *you*. Chapter 4 identifies and explores the nonlegal risks that derivatives pose, some of which may surprise you.

Chapter 5 tells the sad tale of a major Japanese metal trading house whose head trader cost it over $2 billion in business losses and the ignominy of paying the largest penalty ever assessed by a U.S. regulator, all for activity confined mainly to the United Kingdom and Japan. It explores the international implications of derivatives disasters and how making peace after a calamity may require settling up with a variety of foreign governments.

And different nations may respond to derivatives problems in very different ways, including a political dimension that can create a hostile business climate and sometimes hostile courts as well. Chapter 6 explores how derivatives activity has grown throughout the world, including the evolution of scores of new organized markets in these products, and the cultural and political pitfalls that can be encountered when that business comes under stress.

Chapter 7 will provide some pointers on how to structure your organization's oversight of derivatives activity. There is no single or best way, of course, but this book will disclose what seems to work, as well as some structures that, while they look good, usually fail miserably. Because your organization's health, not to mention your own future (promotions, raises, options, even your job), is at stake, this chapter warrants your special attention.

Professional market regulators and banking supervisors have studied derivatives risks very carefully in recent years. From that effort has evolved a set of basic principles and analytical methods that are recommended for use in measuring and controlling those exposures. Chapter 8 summarizes the program that is supported by two of the most distinguished international financial supervisory bodies, the Basle Committee on Banking Supervision and the International Organization of Securities Commissions (IOSCO); and Appendix C contains their recommendations on how best to carry out the oversight of derivatives activity.

Chapter 9 looks ahead to the likelihood that major restructuring of the derivatives markets will occur in the immediate years to come. This is important to derivatives managers because current assumptions about external protections now provided by the exchanges or the regulatory community could change or even disappear, leaving derivatives users to fend largely for themselves. On the organized exchanges a strong trend exists to replace large trading floors and crowds with screen-based dealing; this could produce huge redundancies in both personnel and facilities and pose unique problems for the regulators as well. The traditional mind-sets, like distinguishing between "exchange trading" and "over the counter," which now influence both business and legal decisions, may disappear in the years ahead. Technology will almost surely blur these distinctions. It will also reduce substantially the time required to complete a derivatives trade, and the time in which disaster can strike. Proper oversight under those circumstances will require different checks and balances, and Chapter 8 serves as a warning that today's supervisory systems, as good as they are, need constant updating to keep pace with the changing *structure* of the derivatives business.

Chapter 10 will introduce you to the inevitable political dimension of the derivatives business, identifying who at the federal and state levels can have the greatest influence on—and can do the greatest damage to—those who serve or participate in these markets. This subject is in huge flux at the moment; federal departments and agencies are quarreling over how—or even *whether*—to police this activity, while various states seem eager to devour whatever the Feds do not keep to themselves. Meanwhile the media continue to foment public relations problems for the derivatives community that can influence governmental decisions. Ignore Washington or the state capitol (or the press) at your peril!

Just a lot of "scare tactics"? Lawyers are notorious for that. To overcome that suspicion, I have included in Appendix A the summary report prepared by the Bank of England about the collapse in 1995 from derivatives losses of the "Queen's bank," Baring's, after centuries of successful operations through revolutions, wars, and famines. It stands as a stark testament to what can happen when derivatives trading breaks loose of prudential controls. By the way, although Baring's was finally rescued from oblivion by another firm, few of Baring's key executives kept their jobs.

CHAPTER 1

What Are Derivatives?

It is difficult to imagine a word that conveys *less* information about these complex financial instruments than "derivative." To those who live in the real world, that term denotes something that has been extracted or refined from a specific source, while "derivatives" as used by financial engineers have only a hypothetical connection with the asset, event, or other benchmark that they interact with. Instead, these derivatives involve a form of *pretending* an ownership or other interest in the benchmark source and reaping the same economic consequences as if a genuine transaction were occurring. It is "Let's make believe" using real money. The word that better describes derivatives, and which I prefer, is "synthetics."

Because derivatives reflect imaginary events, they can be embellished in many ways. For example, the size of the "transaction" can be magnified or miniaturized to a noncommercial size. The impact of price changes can also be exaggerated ("leveraged") so that, to illustrate, a $1 change in the reference mark might produce a $10 impact. Or the derivative may be given a life cycle that is quite different from the commercial norm. As a consequence, it is possible to inject great volatility and thus great risk in a "trade" which, compared with the normal behavior of the reference mark, would otherwise give no cause for alarm whatsoever.

Derivatives can be broadly classified as either *standardized* or *customized*. Derivatives are designed to be standardized when the objective is to offer the widest appeal to potential participants by keeping the specifications as simple as possible and by making the ability to trade out of ("offset") a prior transaction easier. Where a large number of transactions, some to buy and some to sell, enjoy this "fungibility," it is far easier to do a closing countertrade with either the same or a new counterparty. Standardized derivatives are the norm on the organized exchanges where simplicity and ease of offset are critical.

Derivatives are customized in response to very specific needs of an end user. As previously noted, derivatives can be designed with great flexibility, including unusual durations, quantities, price leverage, etc. Exchange-traded derivatives are frequently too rigidly structured to accommodate unique needs, but the customized derivatives do very well in that environment. While customized derivatives offer precise responses to users' needs, their uniqueness poses certain other risks:

The dealer is charging a fee. Is it fair and competitive?

I am trying to keep track of what my derivative is worth. Where do I look for accurate data?

If I want to close out the transaction before it expires, can I? If so, how do I know that the price is fair?

Both standardized and customized derivatives have enjoyed huge success. To some degree, they stimulate interest in each other. For instance, a dealer offering a customized derivative may use a similar standardized derivative to reduce its market exposure, that is, to "hedge" against potential losses on the customized instrument. And the availability of this hedging opportunity may encourage the dealer to offer even more customized derivative products. This symbiotic relationship between standardized and customized derivatives appears to have weakened in recent years, however, as dealers have developed other derivative products that can provide hedging protection without using the exchanges' standardized offerings.

The remainder of this chapter will discuss four generic types of derivatives that constitute the lion's share of the business today. These include *futures contracts, options, swaps,* and *hybrid instruments.* Only one class of these derivatives—futures contracts—is subject to heavy federal regulation, while some options are and some are not pervasively regulated, as discussed in Chapter 3. In addition, this chapter discusses *forward contracts*, which began humbly enough as simply a deal in which performance was deferred for a while but which have now mutated to where performance may not ever occur.

At the end of this chapter I will introduce another word that, like "derivatives," seems ill-suited to being understood even among intelligent people. It began life with a useful purpose: to describe then-traded derivatives in a generic way. But as derivatives have expanded into any and all things of value, it has become a nuisance and a distraction. The term is "commodity," and it is relegated to the end of this chapter because it deserves no higher billing.

FUTURES CONTRACTS

In any transaction where the equivalent of real ownership occurs without actually acquiring *anything*, a "futures contract" may be present. Figure 1-1 depicts the structure of a standardized, exchange-traded futures contract.

True ownership typically means that both the joy of gain and the agony of loss in value are borne in equal measure. Price movements, therefore, have a *symmetrical* impact on gain and loss.

FIGURE 1-1
Futures Transaction

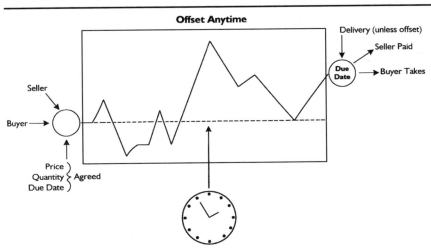

FIGURE 1-2

Futures Contract Economic Profile (Buyer/Long Position)

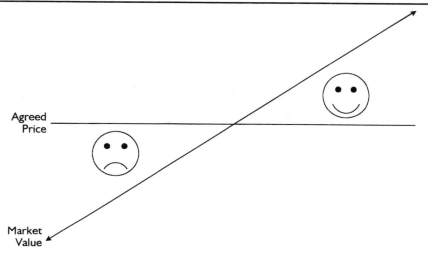

Figure 1-2 illustrates the price behavior of a futures contract from the viewpoint of the buyer.

And while the economic effect is as if ownership actually exists, the "thing" itself almost never emerges. Indeed, the hypothetical "seller" will rarely own it, and the putative "buyer" will seldom receive it. Rather, the outcome is normally reflected in a *cash payment* from one party to the other based upon market changes during the contract's existence.

Some futures contracts obligate the seller (called a "short") to actually deliver to the buyer (called a "long") a specified quantity of the "thing" during a stated month in the future.[1] But because the futures contract can be traded on the sponsoring exchange, either party can exit the market through a countertrade with the original counterparty or with a stranger at any time until the final delivery period. This "offset" election is taken over 95 percent of the time since the parties' aim is to capture the *economics* of the deal rather

---

1. Do not be confused by the traditional definition of a "futures contract" that speaks in terms of an "obligation" to make or take delivery. In reality, futures contracts rarely result in physical transfer of the underlying thing and should be viewed normally as an effort simply to capture the same *economic results* as if a real transaction had occurred.

than actual ownership. In other futures contracts, delivery is not allowed at all and the contract will always be settled through either an offset in the market (settled in cash) or, at the end, a closing cash settlement between the parties.

Here are several illustrations of futures contracts:

Commodity. A commitment by one party to deliver to the other party 100 ounces of gold having a fineness (purity) of .995 during the month of December 1999 at a price of $300 per ounce (physical delivery occurs unless there is market offset).

Equity index. A commitment by one party to the other to pay an amount of money equal to $100 times the numerical level of the Standard & Poor's 500 stock index at inception, with payment due in the month of May 1999 (no stocks are delivered; cash settlement only).

Interest rate. A commitment by one party to deliver to the other party a U.S. Treasury bond having a face (redemption) value of $100,000 for $99,500 (current value)[2] during the month of June 2000 (book entry).

The economic theory behind a futures contract is that the "long" (buyer) is deemed to profit if prices increase while the contract is held, because had a real transaction been completed, the long could acquire the "thing" at the lower contracted price and re-sell in the market at the higher prevailing price. Conversely, the "short" (seller) is deemed to profit if prices decline during that period, because had there been a real trade, the short could have acquired the "thing" at the lower prevailing price and delivered it at the higher contracted price.

Futures contracts are standardized products that generally do not exist (not lawfully, at least) except under the auspices of an organized exchange. It is the exchange and its economists that design the futures contracts and decide on their specifications. A futures contract comes into existence every time a long and a short make a trade together on the market. This may result in an

---

2. The price of bonds declines as interest rates rise in order that all bonds yield the same rate. For example, a 6 percent bond that originally sold for $1,000 (yielding $60 per year) would fall to roughly $925 if interest rates increased to 6.5 percent so that the $60 in annual interest equates with a 6.5 percent return on the investment.

increase in the overall number of futures contracts in existence, or
it may shrink the "open interest" if the new contract offsets a preexisting position of the parties. As a result, the number of futures
contracts that can exist at any given time is theoretically infinite
(unlike, say, a listed common stock where the number of outstanding shares is fixed).

Using either an open outcry or electronic trading system, the
exchange conducts a market in its futures contracts which enables
buyers and sellers to enter and exit almost at will. The exchanges
themselves do not trade, however. They are analogous to an airport
where facilities are provided for *others* to conduct their business.
The exchanges also provide two additional services. First, they police their members and dealers against misconduct and dangerous
financial practices. Second, they generally maintain a facility, called
a "clearinghouse," which guarantees the financial aspects of every
completed futures transaction there; no participant in the market
needs to worry about a default on the part of any other player.

OPTIONS

An option does not behave like a futures contract. An option gives
one party an opportunity for a certain period of time to complete
the transaction but also a right to walk away if completion would
not be profitable. For this flexibility, the party pays a fee to the counterparty called a "premium," which is usually only a small fraction
of the overall face value of the trade. As a result, the most that the
party can lose by failing to complete the transaction is the premium
already paid (plus any commissions paid to brokers or other service costs), while that party's potential profit may be unlimited if favorable market movements occur. The structure of an exchange-
traded option (which can be exercised at any time, known as
"American-style") is depicted in Figure 1-3.

An option, therefore, has *asymmetrical* economic behavior, as
can be illustrated by Figure 1-4.

Examples of options (using the same asset classes as for the
futures contract illustrations) would be:

Commodity. A right, but not an obligation, of the option
purchaser to sell (if a "put") or to buy (if a "call") 100 ounces

FIGURE 1-3
Options Contract Structure ("Amercian Style")

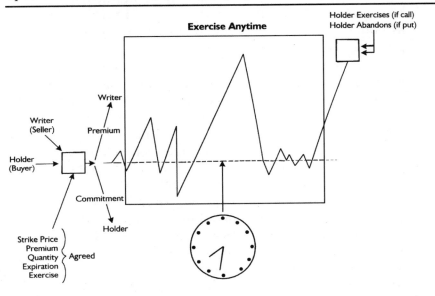

FIGURE 1-4
"Call" Option—Economic Profile

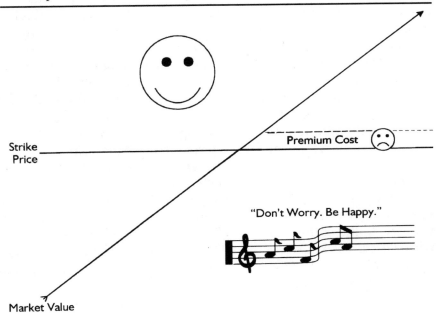

of .995 gold for $300 an ounce during a specified time period or on a selected date; at expiration the right is lost if it has not been exercised. The counterparty receives a premium at inception for agreeing to stand by to perform if the option purchaser decides to exercise the right.

Equity index. A right, but not an obligation, of the option purchaser to sell (if a put) or to buy (if a call) an amount equal to $100 times the Standard & Poor's 500 index level at inception (or other agreed price) for a defined period or on a specified date; at expiration the right is lost if it has not been exercised. A premium payment is received by the counterparty for agreeing to stand by to perform if the option purchaser decides to exercise the right.

Interest rates. A right, but not an obligation, of the option purchaser to sell (if a put) or to buy (if a call) a $100,000 U.S. Treasury bond at a price of $99,500 (or other agreed price) for an express period of time or on a particular date; at expiration the right is lost if it has not been exercised. Again, a premium is paid and the counterparty must be prepared to perform during the option's life if exercise occurs.

Special jargon applies to options as with futures contracts. The party with the flexibility to abandon the transaction is called a "holder" of the option. The counterparty, who receives a premium but must be ready to pay any and all profits accruing to the holder from favorable market movements, is known as the "writer" of the option. Each option identifies a price at which the option begins to be profitable, called the "strike" or "exercise price." And since options have a limited life span, the last opportunity to exercise is called the "expiration date." Some options can be exercised any time before they expire and are referred to as "American-style" options, while the term "European-style" applies when exercise is confined to a certain date (e.g., the final day).

Options have appeal in those situations where a holder wants to enjoy any beneficial market developments but without becoming exposed to the entire "downside" risk. An option benefitting from price *increases* is known as a "call" option (see Figure 1-4), while an option gaining from *falling* prices is referred to as a "put" option and is depicted in Figure 1-5.

FIGURE 1-5
"Put" Option—Economic Profile

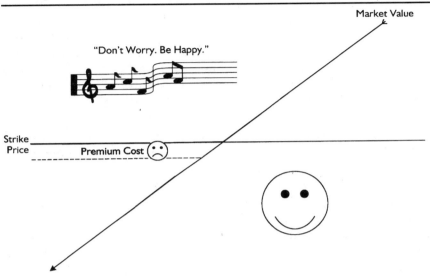

The "call" is commonly used to generate gain in situations where the holder may need to conduct actual purchases while costs are rising, whereas the "put" is often used to generate gain in situations where the holder may need to make actual sales in a falling market. The resulting profit from the options cushions the effect of paying higher prices (in the call scenario) or selling at lower prices (in the put scenario). Options are also useful for these purposes when the actual amount of any real purchases or sales is not known; the premiums paid for protection tend to be small even when "too many" options are acquired. And, of course, options can be used simply to play the market.

The greater risk on an option clearly rests with the writer who must be prepared to pay the full amount of any market profits owed to the holder. In the case of a call option, a writer may actually acquire the underlying "thing" so that its own appreciation will cover any gain owed to the holder. For the writer of a put option, however, other hedging measures may be needed to provide funds covering the difference between low current market value and the higher strike price owed to the holder.

SWAPS

While futures contracts and options have existed for centuries, the "swap agreement" is a creature of the 1980s and emerged from the banking community, not from the organized exchanges. It entails an exchange between two parties of payments calculated with reference to different benchmarks. Among the earliest "swaps" was a switch of payment obligations between a party having fixed-rate debt and a party with floating-rate debt. For example, suppose that Mega Motors, having a very high credit rating, can easily borrow funds from the banks at a fixed rate of, say, 8 percent per annum. But Start-Up Corp., with a far lower credit rating, cannot borrow except at floating rates, which, say, are currently 9 percent per annum. However, the treasurer of Mega thinks that interest rates are about to decline substantially, even to below the 8 percent rate that it is locked into. Meanwhile, the chief financial officer of Start-Up fears that interest rates are about to soar and that its borrowing costs will rise dramatically. These very different concerns can be addressed through a swap between Mega and Start-Up in which Mega agrees to pay to Start-Up any increase in the floating rate above 9 percent while Start-Up agrees to pay to Mega any decline in interest rates below 8 percent. This assures Mega that it will enjoy any fall in interest rates even though its real borrowing costs have not changed, while Start-Up is protected against the higher cost resulting from a rise in the floating rate on its borrowings.

As with other derivatives, swap transactions are hypothetical in nature. In the example, Mega did not change its actual borrowings, nor did Start-Up. In all likelihood, their lending banks knew nothing about this swap. Rather, they simply agreed to *pretend* that a change had occurred and to pay each other accordingly. To round out the transaction, of course, the interest rate payments would have to be related to some amount of hypothetical "borrowing" which the parties will agree to use in their payment calculations, say, $100 million (called the "notional value" of the swap). Thus, if interest rates were to decline to 6 percent, Start-Up would pay Mega the equivalent of $2 million per annum (8 percent − 6 percent = 2 percent x $100 million). Conversely, if interest rates were to rise to 10 percent, Mega would pay Start-Up the equivalent of $1 million per annum (10 percent − 9 percent = 1 percent x $100 million). The payment dates are also negotiable, so they may occur annually,

FIGURE 1-6
Interest Rate "SWAP" (Economic Profile)

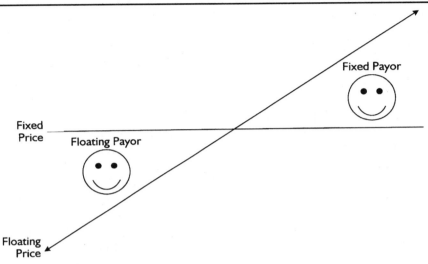

quarterly, monthly, or at any other agreed interval. Occasionally (but not often), there may be a single "bullet" payment involved.

Swaps are not limited to interest rate use although they originated there. Today, swaps are used in connection with foreign currencies, commodities, securities, and a variety of other environments, as discussed below. Figure 1-6 illustrates the typical consequences of an interest rate swap.

Foreign currency swaps are commonly used to reduce an importer/exporter's exposure to a strengthening or weakening of currencies in which its business is conducted. The *Wall Street Journal* and other business publications frequently report that companies' quarterly earnings have been impacted by changes in the exchange rate of currencies in which they must deal. A currency swap transfers that risk between the two parties. To illustrate, suppose Nippon Industries fears that its U.S. sales, made in U.S. dollars ($US), will suffer if the $US weakens against the Japanese yen (¥). On the other hand, Appalachian Produce worries that its sales to Japan, made in ¥, will suffer if the ¥ weakens against the $US. To protect themselves, Nippon and Appalachian agree to exchange between them a certain fixed number of ¥ (say, 1 million) for a fixed number of $US (say, $8,333), or a current exchange rate of 120¥:1$US.[3] Even if the ¥ increases in value relative to the $US, Appalachian is obliged only to pay $8,333 for the ¥, while a strengthening of the $US against the ¥ does not increase the number of ¥ owed by Nippon. In effect, Nippon profits when higher-valued $US are received for lower-valued ¥, and Appalachian profits when higher-valued ¥ are received for lower-valued $US. These profits help to cushion ("hedge against") the effect of changes in the $US/¥ exchange rate on the real business being done by Nippon and Appalachian.

A commodity swap is designed to operate similarly to an interest rate swap in that one party agrees to pay a fixed price for the agreed notional quantity of the commodity while the other party agrees to pay whatever is the market value of the commodity on the payment date. For instance, suppose Global Oil is concerned that crude oil prices will decline while Paradise Cruises, a voracious consumer of energy products, fears that crude oil prices will increase. Global and Paradise could enter into a crude oil swap where Paradise agrees to pay to Global a fixed price for a notional amount of crude oil while Global agrees to pay to Paradise the going market price of crude oil on a payment date. If the fixed price to be paid by Paradise were set at, say, $20 per barrel, Paradise would profit from a rise in crude oil prices above that level (cushioning its higher real fuel costs) while Global would profit if crude oil prices fell below $20 (making up for the lower revenues from its real sales of crude oil).

For a graphic illustration of the structure of interest rate, currency, and commodity swaps, see Figure 1-7.

Another type of swap involves payments referenced to changes in the value of a security or security index. This type of swap typically involves one party paying a rate of interest on a notional amount, which may be fixed or floating, while the other party pays some or all of the results achieved by the security or security index. Where that payment includes both price appreciation and dividends or other distributions, it is referred to as a "total-return" security

---

3. A currency swap may also provide for the periodic payment of interest on a notional amount of currency, to be paid in different currencies. In the illustration, Nippon might make quarterly ¥ interest payments to Appalachian while Appalachian makes quarterly $US interest payments to Nippon at a preagreed rate on the notional amount (which need not be the same for both parties).

FIGURE 1-7
"SWAP" Structure

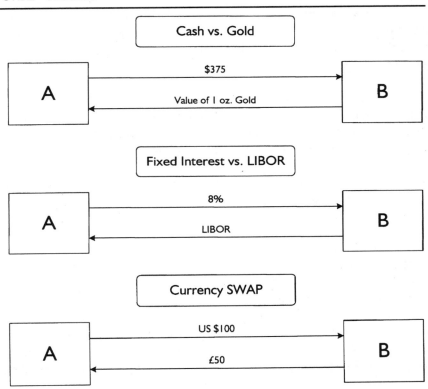

swap. The party paying interest benefits when the payments received on the security or index exceed that interest, while the other
party gains when the interest payment is greater than the results of
the security or index. For reasons discussed in Chapter 3, security-
based swaps can pose special regulatory problems in addition to the
risks commonly associated with swap transactions generally.

Swap transactions are purely private arrangements. As a consequence, certain safeguards present on the organized exchanges
do not exist. There is no clearinghouse,[4] for example, to act as a

---

4. Various proposals have surfaced to create a clearinghouse for swaps and it is expected
    that this goal will eventually be achieved. As noted in Chapter 3, however, this may
    require regulatory approval.

financial guarantor of swap transactions; close attention must therefore be paid to the creditworthiness of one's counterparty, and it is not uncommon for one or both of the parties to demand a deposit of collateral to secure the resulting obligations. In addition, there may not be a resale market for the swap; early termination or transfer will often depend on the consent of one's counterparty.

And there are risks and difficulties in calculating the moving value of a swap; even though a pricing benchmark may be agreed to, a disruption in the underlying activity or in price reporting can make valuation very problematical. At this writing, for instance, the swap dealers are struggling with what to do about long-term currency swaps in present European currencies like the French franc and the German deutsche mark if the single Euro replaces them before those swaps expire.

Like other derivatives, swaps can be designed in a variety of ways. The examples given above assume that the parties wish to realize the entire price change that occurs within the swap. But this is not always the case. In some instances, the parties may be willing to accept some of the price risk, but not beyond a certain point. Or the parties may want the swap to protect them only if prices move beyond a certain range from their present levels. In the first instance, the parties may agree that payments will be made only up to a specified price increase (a "cap") or down to a specific price decline (a "floor"), as depicted in Figure 1-8. In the second example, the parties agree that no payments will be made unless price changes exceed an agreed band (a "collar"), as shown in Figure 1-9.

In economic terms, the parties in both cases have added *options* to their swap. In the cap/floor configuration, it is as if the party who would otherwise suffer from unlimited price increases is given a call option at the capped level, entitling it to keep any further gains; conversely, the party that would otherwise suffer an unlimited loss is given a put option at the floor level, shifting any further loss to the other party. In the case of a collared swap, it is as if the parties exchange options at the starting point that allow each to keep the early results, with the swap payments kicking in only after the uncovered price change has been exceeded.

In addition, parties may agree that one of them can activate a swap with the other upon the happening of a certain event or

FIGURE 1-8
Swap with "Cap" and "Floor"

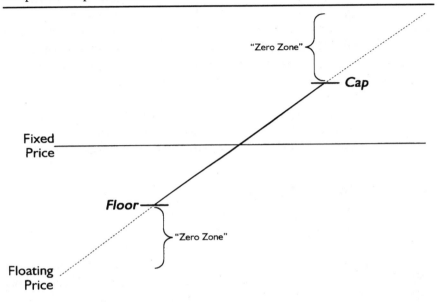

FIGURE 1-9
Swap with "Collar"

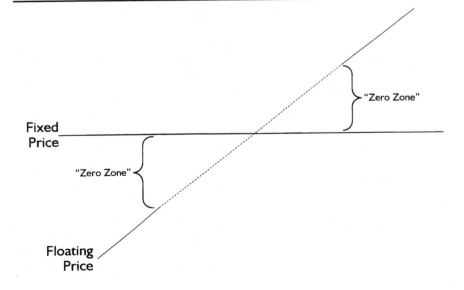

condition. This type of contingent swap, which may never come into existence unless the precondition occurs, is known as a "swaption."

The economic behavior of simple swaps is very similar to that of futures contracts. Payments tend to be generally symmetrical (a change in value benefits one side while burdening the other in roughly equal measure), and the outcome is a cash settlement rather than delivery of that to which the transaction was benchmarked (e.g., loans, ¥, or crude oil). As a consequence, a lively debate has taken place about whether swaps should be viewed and regulated as futures contracts, an outcome that is shown in Chapter 3 to threaten the very existence of the swaps business under current law.

HYBRID INSTRUMENTS

The term "hybrid instrument" has been coined to identify a variety of financial instruments whose price behavior is affected by an independent reference point. Usually, the basic instrument will be a debt security like a medium-term note or a bank product such as a certificate of deposit. It will have the usual original face value and will normally carry a stated interest rate—so far, a pretty typical security. But it is also linked or indexed to something else, so that the *real* principal value and/or the *real* interest rate can change— perhaps dramatically—depending on what happens at that external reference point. For example, imagine a fruit stand selling watermelons geared to the price of Microsoft common stock.

An early example of a hybrid instrument was a certificate of deposit offered by a West Coast bank where the principal due for repayment at maturity could rise above the stated amount or fall below it depending on what happened to the price of gold during the CD's life. A decline in gold prices meant a return of less than the face value of the CD, while a rise in gold prices yielded more than the face value. In effect, the bank offered depositors a chance indirectly to play the gold market through a vehicle that would ordinarily be viewed as a conservative investment. This transaction is depicted in Figure 1-10.

Since then, hybrid instruments have been created to respond to myriad external influences. Many hybrid instruments are linked to changes in the value of specified assets like gold (as above), crude oil, and even measures of inflation like the Consumer Price Index,

FIGURE 1-10
"Hybrid" Instrument (Gold Principal–Indexed Bonds)

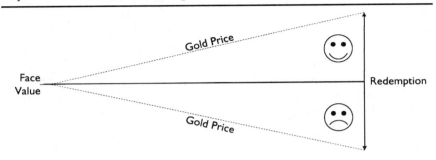

FIGURE 1-11
"Hybrid" Instrument (Hurricane Principal–Indexed Notes)

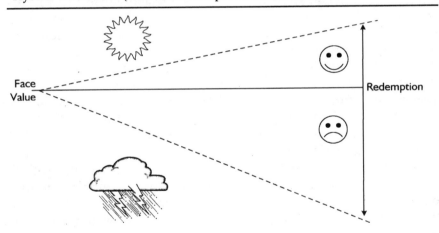

but they appear to be growing ever more exotic. Repayment might be affected, for instance, by changes in the price of the common stock of a completely unrelated company (e.g., notes issued by General Motors that link repayment to the behavior of Intel stock), or relative to the performance of an index of farm products, or even related to weather patterns. Recently, for example, reinsurance companies have sold notes or other securities to institutional investors where principal could be forfeited entirely if an earthquake of a given magnitude were to occur within a defined geographical region. Figure 1-11 depicts the effects of a security whose principal repayment is linked to a weather event.

Among the more recent varieties of hybrid instrument is the "credit derivative." This book speaks at length about how derivatives can *create* myriad risks because of their market volatility, leverage, illiquidity, or other features, but the credit derivative is an instrument designed and used for the *reduction* of a risk. Banks and other lenders, for instance, face the danger of repayment defaults by borrowers. To mitigate this concern, some major lenders have issued notes to investors with attractive interest rates that may fail to repay the principal at maturity if the issuer's loan defaults rise above a specified percentage; in other words, the investors provide a form of credit "insurance" by forfeiting their own funds to make up for the lender-issuer's bad loans.

When repayment on a hybrid instrument can exceed the face value as well as fall short of it, it bears a resemblance to a futures contract and, as noted in Chapter 3, certain regulatory considerations apply. Like a futures contract, it is unlikely that the issuer will have to offer any special compensation such as an above-market yield in order to lure investors; after all, the instrument holds out the possibility of windfall profits to the investor as well as a risk of loss. But for hybrid instruments where the investor has a risk of loss but little or no "upside" potential, as in the earthquake bond described earlier, expect to see an interest rate well above the market rate for ordinary debt.

Opposite the investor is the issuer, of course, and its motivation warrants examination as well. If the defined contingency does not materialize, the issuer will find itself paying more for financing than if it had issued plain debt instead. But the issuer frequently has objectives other than financing in mind. In the case of a note linked to an unrelated company's stock value, the issuer may own a substantial block of that stock as an investment, or as the result of a failed tender offer or hostile takeover, or due to some other corporate development. By issuing the notes, that issuer has effectively transferred to investors the risk of a market decline in the stock, and without having to sell a single share. Or an issuer engaged in the energy business may sell oil-linked bonds so that investors share the risk of an adverse change in oil prices (i.e., the principal on the notes that the issuer retains at maturity compensates for the oil losses). Similarly, in the case of earthquake bonds, shifting the risk of loss to the investors (into the "capital markets") may be a cheaper way to increase the reinsurance pool than more traditional sources of funds. In other words, hybrid instruments afford an issuer the opportunity to hedge against certain commercial risks by using investors' funds to cover business losses.

Hybrid instruments can also have indirect appeal. Certain hybrid structures may be eligible for more favorable tax treatment than applies to ordinary debt. And investors who operate under guidelines or strictures prohibiting speculation in commodities or other assets, but who are allowed to trade "securities," may try to use hybrid instruments to satisfy the latter requirement but enjoy the excitement of playing a wilder market.

Therefore, all instruments bearing the generic title of "securities" or "notes" or "certificates of deposit" are not the same. Today, investing in a money market fund or a seemingly conservative fixed-income mutual fund can involve risky hybrid instruments that may make the venture far more volatile than their titles suggest. No longer may one assume that these investments are purged of all speculative behavior; on the contrary, as Orange County, California, learned the hard way through ignominious bankruptcy, it is vitally important to look beyond the classification given to an investment and understand what *really* controls its performance.

FORWARD CONTRACTS

A decade ago I would not have thought to include forward contracts within the family of derivatives. Historically, forward contracts were simply routine sales where final performance was delayed to accommodate some event or situation. But these instruments have evolved into highly tradable financial products that may or may not satisfy a merchandising need. Because many of them are ultimately settled in cash, they can present the same hedging and speculating opportunities as other forms of derivatives. As discussed in Chapter 3, the CFTC has modified its regulatory posture on forward contracts, permitting far greater design flexibility than in previous time. Had this not occurred, the legality of today's forward contracts might have been brought under serious challenge.

In their basic structure, forward contracts involve entering into an agreement with the understanding that it will not be carried out immediately. The delay in performance means, especially if a price has been agreed on, that the delivered item(s) may have become more or less valuable during the lag period. For the party having the performance obligation, a decline in price offers an opportunity to acquire the thing later at a lower price to be delivered at the contract's higher price. For the intended recipient, a rise in price during the lag period means the ability to resell at an above-contract price. In economic terms, a forward contract closely resembles a *futures contract* as depicted in Figure 1-1 and offers the same profit/loss profile. Now that the CFTC allows (on conditions) a forward contract to be cash-settled and for actual performance to be avoided, these instruments can compete directly with the far more heavily regulated futures contracts.

WHAT DO YOU MEAN "COMMODITY"?

Derivatives existed for many years only on tangible assets like grains and metals. Not surprisingly, they were commonly associated with the term "commodity" as a result. For several generations the moniker seemed to fit quite well. But the advent of derivatives on financial assets, followed by even more exotic instruments, made reference to "commodities" a clumsy anachronism. And so we stopped using the term, right? Not in the laws and regulations affecting this activity.

By 1974, derivatives existed in foreign currencies and were under development in a variety of interest rate products. Recognizing that the conventional meaning of "commodity" no longer fit, Congress faced two choices. It could strike the word from the laws and regulations. Or it could redefine the term so broadly that it would cover almost anything. The latter course was pursued in the end, causing "commodity" to mean in the derivatives world something painfully foreign to normal language usage. As a result, market users and a great many lawyers became entrapped by this fuzzy term, which, in almost any other context, could not possibly be associated with their activities.

Originally, the word "commodity" was defined for regulatory purposes to mean a long list of farm products. When financial derivatives surfaced in the 1970s, Congress added the phrase "and all other goods and articles . . . and all services, rights, and interests" in which regulated derivatives exist or later came into being. Just about *anything* of value would drop into one or more of those vast categories, including securities, other financial instruments, and even intangibles like stock indexes or inflation measures. As a practical matter it became necessary to assess every situation in reverse of the logical order: Begin by deciding whether the instrument itself is a regulated derivative, and if so, there is a high probability that whatever it reflects is a "commodity."

The expansion of derivatives into many sectors of economic life is a good thing; dragging behind the word "commodity" is not. Among the general population, none of the following would likely be associated with the term and yet it applies as a matter of regulatory law:

- Tradable credits issued by the government as part of its emissions control program
- The Consumer Price Index
- An index of bankruptcy filings
- Claims filed by insureds after a natural disaster
- The Standard & Poor's 500 stock index
- An index of crop *yields* (not prices)

If regulated derivatives were traded on them, other examples could be commercial rental rates, airline fare prices, medical costs, etc.

What has become evident during the past generation of the derivatives markets is that anything can be traded if it can be valued. This is because derivatives are not hobbled by the need to transfer property or an evidence of ownership; a payment of price changes ("cash settlement") will do nicely. Perhaps the greatest challenge lies in finding a method of valuation that all participants have confidence in. Once overcome, however, derivatives can be readily created. One of the fastest-growing areas for derivatives at this time relates to valuing *credit risk*. According to *Swaps Monitor*, the current annual growth rate for credit derivatives is above 300 percent. One example would be an offering of debt securities (e.g., notes) by a lending institution that will not be repaid in full if loan defaults exceed a specified level; another would be a swap agreement requiring the counterparty (who will receive specified payments) to transfer a certain sum of money if and when that level is reached.

As any semanticist would expect, using an inapt word like "commodity" to describe intangible and ephemeral things, including raw mathematical formulas, can lead to bizarre results and necessitates an abundance of distinctions, exceptions, and the like. It would be cruel to go that far in this book. It should suffice to understand that the term encompasses far more than it has any right to; the application of common sense in this context simply must be suspended.

CHAPTER 2

Why Do They Exist?

Derivatives have existed for centuries. One of the earliest recorded instances involved trading in Japanese rice on the Dojima Rice Exchange in the 1700s, although it is quite likely that some forms of derivatives have existed throughout the world's commercial history. In the United States, the first organized derivatives market emerged in Chicago in the mid-1800s when the Chicago Board of Trade, which had long been a key market for physical grain trading, refined the process to allow grain futures trading as well. After that, it seemed that every significant city in the country wanted to have its own futures market, but following an inevitable shakeout, only about 10 exchanges have survived. On the international scene, futures and options markets were fairly rare until the 1980s when scores of exchanges were opened throughout Europe, Latin America, and Asia, initially to trade local products like the national government bond but expanding into other areas as opportunities arose. Today, there are roughly 50 foreign derivatives markets in nearly 30 countries.

The evolution of off-exchange derivatives first manifested itself in a dramatic way during the 1980s and, while this makes the over-the-counter segment "young" by comparison with the organized exchanges, it has grown at light speed ever since. According to statistics maintained by the over-the-counter dealers' trade association, the International Swaps and Derivatives Association, the notional value of all such derivatives in 1996 exceeded $25 *trillion* across 83 dealers worldwide, with about three-fourths of that amount represented by interest rate swaps.

THE HEDGING INSTINCT

It is fair to say that derivatives markets did not emerge simply to satisfy the gambling habits of the human race. A multitude of vehicles has always been available for that purpose, most of which are far more accessible and less intimidating than the derivatives markets. Rather, most derivatives markets arose from the desire of the business community to *reduce* their existing commercial or financial risks. Of course, because those risks could not simply be wished away or even eliminated, there would have to be other people who were willing to accept a transfer of those risks. In some cases, the transferees were other businesspeople for whom holding that risk also reduced their exposure (e.g., where they normally faced the *opposite* danger so that the new risk neutralized it). But these counterparties would not always be conveniently available, so the system had to admit true punters as well who, to put it impolitely, bet on the direction or velocity of prices. For them, the derivatives markets were simply part of their gambling menu, along with Monte Carlo and Las Vegas.

A classic illustration of this phenomenon was the grain market as it existed in the 1800s. Farm production is necessarily cyclical; at one time of the year (harvest) the countryside is awash in grain, while nine months later it may be a scarce and expensive commodity. When grain was delivered from the fields into Chicago, where lucky sellers would see their harvest loaded onto boxcars for shipment to the eastern cities, the glut usually meant very low prices and, in bumper years, surpluses that often rotted on Chicago's streets. Buying or selling in advance of harvest was risky and very difficult, so most producers simply came to Chicago and took their chances.

In time, however, merchants began to accept the idea of buying "forward" before the physical grain arrived, as it assured, especially in poor years, that they would have a reliable supply of grain available to them for resale. But they also faced the risk that the forward prices that they were committed to pay for the grain would be above-market when delivery occurred, meaning not only that they would overpay for the grain, but that they might have to resell it at a loss. At first, this problem was addressed by a new class of *faux-merchants* who would offer a second forward contract to the original buyer that would shift to them the risk of falling prices by, in effect, offering to acquire the same grain at a price that would not be affected by a decline in the market. The faux-merchant's interest, of course, was in enjoying any rise in grain prices should it occur. But the original buyer as well as the faux-merchant was really interested only in the *economics* of the trade; the original buyer would rather sell to his regular customers, and the faux-merchant would rather not have to handle the grain at all.

Eventually, acting as a faux-merchant became a profession, and forward grain contracts were traded not only with true merchants but among the faux-merchants themselves. An informal "market" resulted which evolved into a futures market once a mechanism was developed to allow one commitment to offset another. From about 1859, the Chicago Board of Trade operated as an efficient futures market and completed its maturation when a clearinghouse guarantee system was added early in the 20th century.

The grain trade's pricing problems were really no different from those of any other segment of the economy, although the cyclical nature of production tended to underscore them. In later years, futures contracts would be created to serve the price hedging needs of dozens of industries ranging from energy to lending, precious metals to foreign currencies, and insurance to pollution abatement.

A parallel development on the exchanges occurred in options which proved to be controversial, perhaps because the low premium cost of buying options attracted the more vulnerable members of the general public. Options on farm products were effectively banned in the 1930s, and most other options were prohibited in the late 1970s. While these restrictions have been relaxed in recent years, a legal thicket still exists when dealing in options on any commodity.

Meanwhile, in the early 1970s there emerged a central options market in *securities*, the Chicago Board Options Exchange, which replaced an informal (and small) network of so-called "put and call dealers" located principally in New York City. The similarity of the market's name to that of the Chicago Board of Trade is no coincidence—it was created by the latter and represented an early manifestation of the idea that "derivatives" outside the traditional commodity business both were needed and could be phenomenally successful. Several years later, when the Chicago Board of Trade offered the first *futures contracts* on securities, the migration of derivatives into the securities world was completed. As in other cases, options and futures on securities were intended to provide protection against adverse market swings, although their speculative use was neither limited nor discouraged. An ancillary benefit was that issuers of securities, including the U.S. government, could often complete their offerings to investors in greater volume or at better prices because the investors could now hedge their price risk by taking options or futures positions in those securities rather than by bidding lower or in less size for the securities to "self-insure" against that danger.

The off-exchange derivatives business which took root in the 1980s was likewise driven by a *fear* of risk, rather than by a thirst to gamble. The same risk-averse parties that used the organized exchanges were often presented with standardized instruments that did not fit hand in glove with their specific (sometimes unique) needs. The standardized futures contract or option might be too big (or too small), might have a duration that is too long (too short), or might relate to a benchmark or asset not quite the same as the thing in which the party is dealing. The banking community, recognizing that it could construct a better hedge for clients through customized, even one-off, instruments wasted no time in designing these new derivatives. As the statistics earlier in this chapter show, the over-the-counter derivatives business has been a bonanza.

Derivatives offer price protection in an especially ingenious way. They allow a party having real, inescapable commercial risks to largely *neutralize* them by acquiring an instrument that will profit from the self-same events that inflict losses in the commercial arena. As depicted in Figure 2-1, a *futures contract* will generate gain at the same time that the commercial transaction is losing money, offering a sort of "insurance policy" that can be cashed in whenever business results are negative. Of course, insurance is never free, and while the classical premium is not charged in a futures transaction, the holder must forfeit any *favorable* price developments in order to be protected from negative events. Economists frequently refer to this balance of risk and reward as a "zero sum game."

FIGURE 2-1
"Long" Futures Hedge (Economic Profile)

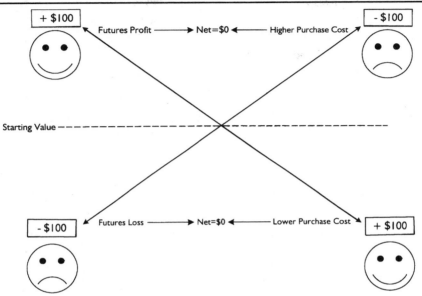

With *options*, however, forfeiture of future gains need not be the cost of protection. As discussed in Chapter 1, the holder of an option incurs only the cost of a "premium" fee to the writer in exchange for the right to enjoy every cent of favorable price movement. If prices move in the opposite direction, the holder does not incur any losses; the option will expire, and the premium will be all (other than service costs) that the holder can lose. For example, a party who is concerned that prices will rise ahead of needed purchases can acquire call options that will generate profit if that fear materializes; but if prices fall instead, losses are limited to the premium and any service costs (e.g., broker commissions) and the holder can continue to enjoy most of the savings from the price decline. This benefit of options is illustrated in Figure 2-2.

In the case of other derivatives, whether there is symmetrical gain and loss (i.e., forfeiture of all favorable price developments to receive full "downside" protection) depends entirely on their design. A conventional *swap* may have that feature, but, as explained in Chapter 1, the inclusion of a cap or floor, or of a collar, can create substantial asymmetry akin to an option. Similarly, *hybrid*

FIGURE 2-2
"Put" Option Hedge—Economic Profile ("At-The-Money")

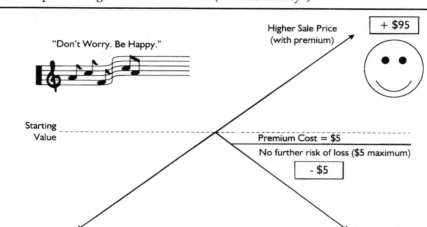

instruments will reward and punish the investor in accordance with their specifications, which can be either symmetrical or asymmetrical. For example, certain of the reinsurance derivatives divide the investor's contribution into "risk capital" to be lost if the defined catastrophe occurs and "nonrisk capital" to be returned to the investor in any event. Allocating the investor's contribution between those two pools can range from 99 percent risk capital to 1 percent risk capital, or anything in between.

Hybrid instruments serve as price hedges by requiring the investor to absorb some of the losses sustained by the issuer in its commercial operations. For reinsurance derivatives, the investors' loss of some or all of their contributions has the practical effect of underwriting claims payments to be made by the issuer to policyholders. In a manufacturing context, a hybrid instrument offered by an aluminum producer and tied to the price of that metal generates funds for the producer in falling markets that reduce the actual impact of lower aluminum prices. And in the financial world, a bank offering linked to interest rates can generate profit when its loan portfolio yields are declining.

HONORING THE "SPECULATOR"

While the driving force for derivatives has been the desire to *avoid* risk, derivatives do nothing to *eliminate* that danger. What derivatives do is to transport the risk from here to there, and often the "there" is an unabashed speculator who is willing to bet that the hedger's worries are unfounded and, indeed, that good things will happen instead. These voluntary risk takers are frequently reviled as avaricious, amoral cads who feed on the misery of others; any TV news spot showing the frenzy occurring on the floor of a futures market after a tragedy or disaster will only reinforce that view. In the 30 years I've been around the derivatives business, however, I have found most speculators to be warm and decent people who simply want to make a living like everyone else. While few of them would suggest that their motives are charitable, the reality is that they free our major companies and institutions from vast amounts of risk that could otherwise threaten their existence or, at a minimum, raise the cost of their goods and services significantly.

A recent example is the interest among institutional investors in hybrid notes or swap agreements on which losses will be incurred if a defined natural disaster occurs. The counterparty will usually be an insurance company or a provider of reinsurance coverage that, in this way, engages in a risk-reducing "hedging" strategy for its core business operations. But the institutional investors are under no obligation to take those risks; they do so voluntarily after concluding that the chances of sacrificing their investment are outweighed by the attraction of a much higher yield on the transaction. In this way some of the world's most highly regarded enterprises have worn the mantle of "speculator" from time to time.

Even so, derivatives trading cannot be entirely disassociated with gambling. While it is true that derivatives generally deal with *types* of preexisting risk, they may actually multiply the *quantity* of those risks by creating more derivatives than are necessary simply to transfer outstanding risk from one person to another.

For example, there may be $50 billion worth of a commodity in existence at a given time, but the aggregate value of all derivatives in that commodity may well exceed that amount, perhaps many times over. This may be due to speculative interest in the commodity, or it could result from multiple hedging of the same unit of commodity as it passes through the various stages of production, distribution, processing, and consumption. Perhaps we can take comfort in the fact that the federal regulator will not authorize trading in a derivative under its jurisdiction unless its likely use for hedging can be demonstrated.

CHAPTER 3

Call in the Lawyers

The market risk created by derivatives has made headlines, and for good reason. The well-publicized plights of Baring's Bank, Sumitomo, Procter & Gamble, Long-Term Capital Management, Gibson Greetings, and even Odessa College in Texas are enough to keep any responsible manager on edge. While this book is devoted primarily to addressing how to protect against business risk, we should not underestimate the *legal* thicket that has grown up around the derivatives industry. In this chapter, some of the complexity of complying with the relevant law—indeed, even trying to *identify* what laws apply—is briefly discussed.

Before you draw the conclusion that legal risks and market risks are unrelated, consider what can happen if the law is violated in connection with a derivatives transaction. Yes, you will probably hear from the authorities, and your attorneys will do their best to negotiate a settlement with the government that you can live with. But what about your counterparties on all of those derivatives transactions that are now under a legal cloud? They may have the right to walk away from the trades (in legal jargon, to "rescind" the transactions), and if they are losing, it is a fair bet that they will try to do just that. In one actual courtroom drama, a physician-real estate mogul tried to avoid payment of over $25 million to a major Wall Street house claiming that his losing trades were illegal and, as a consequence, the debt was not collectible. And so attention to the legal niceties can make the difference between whether or not your derivatives deals are worth the paper they are written on.

The legal environment for derivatives is complicated by two unusual features. First, it is not always easy to determine what rules and regulations apply, or even which of the various financial regulators controls the process. Second, parts of the derivatives world are pervasively regulated while others are virtually free from any pesky regulation. This unnatural situation has generated keen debate in Congress over whether greater parity should exist, probably by reducing the level of regulation in the first sector at least when it deals with the same types of market participants that are served by the unregulated dealers. As a result, the legal landscape is almost certain to change, and *you should consult your attorneys on a regular basis.*[5]

EXCHANGE-TRADED DERIVATIVES

The exchanges where *futures contracts* and certain *options* are listed for trading have been heavily regulated for many years. The futures markets (including those which trade nonsecurities options) are governed by the federal Commodity Exchange Act which is administered by the U.S. Commodity Futures Trading Commission, or CFTC. This act has been in existence since 1922 (predating even the federal securities laws), and while it originally covered only farm products, today it regulates *anything,* including intangibles such as services that are traded through a regulated vehicle. Since 1974, state laws that once also governed this activity have been largely preempted in favor of a single, uniform national regulatory policy. The CFTC has promulgated many hundreds of rules dictating how this business must be conducted. For present purposes, the most important rules (which will be reiterated again and again) are these:

> *No futures contract can be bought or sold except on or under the rules of a CFTC-licensed exchange!*

and

> *Futures contracts on individual corporate securities (e.g., IBM stock) are forbidden.*

---

5. This book does not and is not intended to constitute legal advice.

In the case of certain nonsecurity *options*, the CFTC has also imposed other restrictions on when, where, and how they may be traded.

The exchanges where securities-based *options* are listed must comply with the federal Securities Exchange Act, which is administered by the U.S. Securities and Exchange Commission, or SEC. Like the CFTC, the SEC has issued many rules governing activity in security options, including the rule that an exchange wishing to list security options must register with it as a national securities exchange. However, unlike the CFTC, the SEC has not confined trading to the licensed stock markets, and a thriving business in security options exists outside the exchanges, known as the over-the-counter, or O-T-C, market. And unlike the CFTC's prohibition against stock futures, there is no ban against options on individual corporate securities.

The SEC's jurisdictional reach also includes certain other types of derivative products, which, in ways, are akin to *hybrid instruments*. Some of these derivatives, such as convertible debt securities ("convertibles"), have been around for generations. Others, such as collateralized mortgage obligations and other asset-backed securities (ABSs), are of more recent vintage. Both convertibles and ABSs cause the security to be valued on the basis of some external benchmark. In the case of convertibles, they are sensitive to changes in the price of the underlying common stock into which the investor may convert the debt security. For ABSs, the price sensitivity relates generally to the payment performance of the underlying assets such as a pool of home mortgages, of auto loans, of credit card repayments, etc. Despite the fact that these instruments have "hybrid" features, the CFTC has left their regulation largely to the SEC.

For participants in exchange-traded derivatives, a lawyer is a necessity because regulation is everywhere. While simple buyers and sellers of exchange-traded derivatives have only a limited number of rules to remember (e.g., don't manipulate the market or exceed any limits on holdings), a danger exists that they could augment their basic trading activity in ways that place them in some one or more categories of persons that must actually register with the regulator and follow a plethora of additional rules. If, for example, a market participant decides to give trading advice to others or to take control of someone else's trading capital, a flood of new requirements (including licensing) can rise up. In general, whenever one undertakes to provide a trading-related service to others, the line has been crossed and more regulatory duties (and costs) are triggered.

So regulation is an unmitigated disaster, right? Not necessarily in this case because regulation by the CFTC generally *preempts* applying other laws or regulations to this activity. With derivatives being offered (or capable of being offered) on just about anything, there are potentially an infinite number of governmental departments and agencies that could take an "interest" in these products. For instance, energy-based derivatives could attract regulation by the U.S. Department of Energy, or the Environmental Protection Agency, or state energy bureaus, etc., or by all of the above. And derivatives linked to risks such as losses from hurricanes (they exist!) could generate action by the various state insurance commissions. But to the extent that the CFTC has jurisdiction over these products and activities, it is essentially *exclusive* and no other regulatory wanna-be can become involved. This helps to assure that (1) policy remains uniform and consistent and (2) the massive costs of complying with many different regulatory demands is avoided.

The O-T-C derivatives, on the other hand, are not CFTC-regulated at this time and do run the risk of someday being smothered by a wave of regulators at the national, state, and local levels. This created a dilemma for O-T-C dealers in the early 1990s when they sought to avoid CFTC regulation for certain swap agreements and hybrid instruments but wished to enjoy at least some features of the CFTC's preemption of other regulators. They were especially concerned that states would invoke their gambling laws (after all, the "winners" and "losers" were determined by the chance outcome of the linked benchmark), which is not a risk with CFTC-regulated activity. Thus, Congress fashioned a Solomon-like solution that exempted these transactions from CFTC regulation *and* stopped states from applying their gambling laws. The bad news for these O-T-C derivatives is that they remain vulnerable to every non-gaming law or regulation that could be applied to them.

Outside the exchange-listed world, in the O-T-C market, the law is murkier in other ways as well. This is due, in part, to the relative newness of many of these derivatives, but, in addition, it arises from the fact that so many O-T-C derivatives have features resembling highly regulated exchange-listed products. As noted in Chapter 1, for example, the basic *swap* behaves economically very similar to a *futures contract*. And many *hybrid instruments* possess characteristics of either a *futures contract* (where the linked benchmark can generate both gain and loss) or an *option* (a gain, or a loss, but not both). Indeed, the resemblance of these O-T-C derivatives to regulated instruments has taken the regulators, and especially the CFTC, to the brink of war with the O-T-C derivatives community.

SWAP AGREEMENTS

The CFTC first expressed its interest in *swaps* in 1987 when it hinted that it might choose to regulate them as *futures contracts*. Such a decision would have been catastrophic; recall that only exchange-traded futures contracts are lawful, whereas all then-existing swaps had been created in the O-T-C market. Recognizing these consequences, the CFTC relented in 1989 and allowed O-T-C swaps to continue so long as they did not grow even more similar to futures. In essence, the CFTC told the swap community:

- *Not* to make swap agreements standardized as to their economic terms (e.g., require negotiation of credit terms)
- *Not* to permit "offset" prior to maturity except with counterparty consent
- *Not* to create a formal margining system or provide a clearinghouse-style guarantee against credit risk
- *Not* to enter swaps with persons who have no business purpose for doing so
- *Not* to market swaps to the general public

If these restrictions were met, however, the CFTC said that conforming swaps "are not appropriately regulated [as futures contracts or options] under the Act," which has been construed to mean that the CFTC will not impose *any* regulatory requirement.

The breadth of that action by the CFTC, which appears fundamentally to have made irrelevant both the Commodity Exchange Act and the CFTC's regulations in the case of conforming swaps, was seen by many observers as allowing eligible swaps to operate without regard to either of futures regulation's two principal tenets: the on-exchange limitation and the ban on stock futures. As a result, private O-T-C swap activity continued apace and a number of *stock*-linked swaps were executed in reliance on this CFTC pronouncement even though they had futures-like characteristics.

The O-T-C swap community was not entirely satisfied, however, with this outcome. The CFTC had expressed its position in the form of a "policy statement" which would not necessarily prevent the courts from taking a different view in litigation nor stop the CFTC itself from changing its mind someday. And this approach left open the question of whether swaps might be attacked as gambling under state laws; while CFTC-regulated products are immune from those laws, the newly unregulated swaps might not be.

An opportunity arose in 1992 for a swap solution to be enacted directly into the Commodity Exchange Act, and the swap dealers quickly seized it. Congress directed the CFTC to grant a formal exemption from most of its regulatory requirements for a variety of instruments (defined as "swaps") where the parties meet a certain (largely institutional or affluent) profile, and the CFTC has issued rules implementing that mandate. In addition to the requirements for eligibility to participate, the CFTC specified that the economic terms of a swap must not be standardized, that the creditworthiness of the parties must remain an important consideration (i.e., credit risk must not be eliminated via a clearinghouse or otherwise), and that there must not be any exchange trading in the swaps. When these conditions were met, the CFTC withdrew from a regulatory role except to prosecute fraud. But unlike the earlier "policy statement," the new law also made clear that state gaming laws remained preempted even for qualifying swaps.

The 1992 legislation, however, prohibited the CFTC from using its exemptive authority under the new provisions to waive the ban on stock futures. As a result, stock-linked swaps may not enjoy the same exemptive relief that other qualified swaps enjoy. Nevertheless, it is widely believed that the CFTC's earlier policy statement, issued in 1989, which was not limited in this way can still be used as a "safe harbor" for stock-linked swaps. Absent a full court test, however, the matter remains open to debate. As a consequence, some swap dealers conduct their stock-linked business abroad.

HYBRID INSTRUMENTS

As noted in Chapter 1, *hybrid instruments* can contain *futures-* or *options*-like features and have also drawn the CFTC's attention for that reason. Again, the CFTC has addressed this issue through a two-stage process occurring in the first phase before the 1992 legislation took effect and, later, using the new law's exemptive powers. From the beginning, the CFTC's position was based primarily on whether the hybrid instrument existed (and was bought) mainly for its value as an investment (e.g., as a loan in the case of a note), or whether its principal attraction was the "play" in the linked benchmark. And the CFTC set about to create certain ways to measure which attribute predominates.

In 1989 and 1990, the CFTC made two decisions on the subject. One pertained to hybrid instruments having *futures*-like features, while the other applied to hybrid instruments having *option*-like characteristics. This distinction was driven by a quirk in the CFTC's authority at that time. It could formally "exempt" *options* under existing law, but it would not have similar authority for *futures* until the 1992 law came into being.

For hybrid instruments containing attributes of a *futures contract*, the CFTC issued a "statutory interpretation" to the effect that an "exclusion from regulation under the Commodity Exchange Act" would be recognized for futures-like hybrid instruments, and that they would not be deemed to be "within the coverage of the Act" if they met the following tests:

- The indexing of the instrument to the benchmark could not exceed a ratio of 1:1 (i.e., the indexing could not have "leverage").
- The amount paid by the holder for the hybrid instrument was all that the holder could lose.
- The interest rate or other yield on the hybrid instrument must not be above 150 percent, nor below 50 percent, of the yield that would exist for an instrument of comparable quality that lacked the indexation feature (e.g., a "plain vanilla" note).
- The feature of the hybrid instrument representing indexation must remain attached to the overall instrument; no severability is permitted.

- When the hybrid instrument was finally settled, it could not use any mechanism by which regulated futures markets conduct delivery on their own futures contracts.
- The hybrid instrument must not be marketed as having the characteristics of a futures contract or option.

These CFTC requirements were designed principally to limit the degree to which qualified hybrid instruments could be used as substitutes or surrogates for conventional futures contracts or options.

This "statutory interpretation" suffered from the same weaknesses as the CFTC's swap "policy statement." A court was not obliged to adopt the CFTC's position if the issue surfaced in litigation, and state gambling laws might apply if the CFTC's withdrawal was upheld. As a result, the derivatives community expressed dissatisfaction with this bootstrap solution as well.

In the case of hybrid instruments having *option*-like features, the CFTC adopted formal exemptive rules in 1989. While some of the restrictions that were applied to futures-type hybrid instruments were reiterated in these rules, the central focus was placed on the extent to which the cost of the hybrid instrument was attributable to its options-type behavior. In effect, the CFTC limited that amount to 40 percent of the instrument's overall value. Computing this percentage required fairly sophisticated mathematics, as befits an agency then run by an economist.

After the 1992 legislation broadened the CFTC's exemptive powers to include futures contracts, the CFTC once again addressed the subject of hybrid instruments. Unlike its earlier effort, however, the CFTC could now adopt formal rules for futures-like hybrid instruments as well, and it did, encompassing both futures- and options-type features (the older option rules were dropped). And like its formal exemption for swaps, the CFTC's new power with respect to hybrid instruments included a preemption of state gaming laws. The new rules adopted most of the requirements contained in the previous "statutory interpretation" but liberalized the fraction of the hybrid instrument's overall value that can be attributed to its futures- or options-based behavior. As a result, that amount was increased from 40 percent of total value to any amount less than 50 percent of total value. The same mathematical complexities are involved, and many attorneys (including the author) routinely send new hybrid instrument proposals to finance academics or proficient mathematicians to "crunch the numbers."

OVER-THE-COUNTER OPTIONS

The CFTC is a factor in the *options* world beyond simply swaps or hybrid instruments having that feature. As noted earlier, there are a number of CFTC restrictions on options activity, arising largely from bad past experiences ranging from perceived disruption of orderly markets to outright sales fraud. Consequently, in general *only* the following nonsecurity options can lawfully be traded in the United States:

- Options listed on a CFTC-licensed exchange
- Options offered solely to persons for commercial purposes
- Options embedded in or that fall within the definition of a CFTC-exempt "swap"
- Options embedded in a CFTC-exempt hybrid instrument

Of course, options on *securities,* as noted earlier, are not affected by these restrictions because they are regulated by the SEC, not the CFTC, and, while the SEC has set its own standards for security options, nothing akin to the CFTC's broad ban exists in the securities world.

FORWARD CONTRACTS

Finally, a word about *forward contracts.* The laws that regulate futures contracts do not generally apply to forward contracts. This is because futures contracts are actively traded instruments with an established market that are usually held for investment or hedging and not as a commercial source or outlet for supplies. Forward contracts, viewed historically, have tended to be simple merchandising arrangements where a transfer of ownership will take place but not until some time in the future. For example, a grain exporter may want to procure a supply now, but to take delivery only after a ship has been chartered to haul it away. Or a building contractor may wish to lock in a supply of copper right away, but to start receiving it only after construction has begun.

For many years, these examples sufficed to illustrate what a forward contract is. As recently as 1985, the CFTC described these instruments as deals where actual delivery "routinely occurs." But in 1990 the CFTC was forced to revisit the matter after a federal court ruled that the North Sea crude oil market (popularly known as the "Brent" market) was actually an illegal futures market because, while each trade was written up as if delivery would occur, the same cargo was actually bought and sold many times and delivery occurred on only about 5 percent of the trades. That ruling effectively expelled all U.S. participants from the Brent market.

The CFTC came to the rescue by issuing a special "statutory interpretation" which stated, in effect, that the absence of delivery will not destroy a transaction's status as an unregulated forward contract provided that it met the following standards:

- The transaction as originally entered must call for actual delivery and in a commercially recognized manner.
- There could not be a "wink and a nod" understanding between the parties that delivery would not take place.
- Only through a subsequent amendment to the original deal, which either side must be free to reject, could delivery be abandoned in favor of a cash settlement.

This appears to be the basic structure used in the Brent market, and as a result, U.S. interests were able to renew their participation in that business. Accordingly, the historical litmus test which was coldly objective (no delivery? not a forward contract) has been displaced by a devotion to form and process. It is for that reason that I have included forward contracts as "derivatives" in this book.

With the CFTC's withdrawal from regulating many of the more popular derivatives in the late 1980s and early 1990s, it appeared that dealers in those financial products had found a virtually regulation-free Promised Land. While there remained the technical possibility of controls by other regulators like the Treasury Department or the Federal Reserve, neither of those agencies views itself as primarily a "regulator," and aggressive oversight of the off-exchange derivatives business by them seemed highly unlikely. But more recent steps at both the SEC and the CFTC suggest that things may be changing.

In December 1997, the SEC announced that it was considering the creation of a new registration (licensing) category under the federal securities laws for "over-the-counter derivatives dealers." The proposal was couched in terms of providing "relief" to existing SEC-regulated securities broker-dealers who found it difficult to conduct an O-T-C derivatives business within their main company. In essence, they would be allowed to form a separate entity and, after SEC licensing, pass the O-T-C business through that vehicle. Was this a rare manifestation of government compassion? Or was this the proverbial "camel's nose under the tent" that would lead eventually to full-bore SEC regulation of the derivatives community?

While the SEC's motivations were being debated, the CFTC delivered to the SEC in February 1998 a strongly worded letter objecting to the SEC's proposed licensing system for O-T-C derivatives dealers. Noting that less than 2 percent (by notional value) of all reported O-T-C derivatives transactions involve instruments that are "securities" under the SEC's regime, the CFTC said that a far larger percentage were or could be treated as futures, options, or other instruments within *its* jurisdiction. Dropping the other figurative shoe, the CFTC also announced that it "is currently evaluating its approach to the oversight of OTC derivatives in light of the tremendous growth and new developments in this market over the past several years." While the Congress took the unusual step in 1998 to prohibit the CFTC from going forward on its O-T-C initiative until at least the second quarter of 1999 (to allow intervening congressional review), effort could resume thereafter. In other words, *maybe* its hands-off policy will continue, but don't count on it. Stay tuned.

PLAYING THE "INSTITUTIONAL" CARD

As originally developed, most legal standards set by the CFTC for exchange-traded derivatives applied equally to large and small market participants. That policy contrasts sharply with the traditional approach of the SEC, which has long recognized a distinction, allowing large institutions and wealthy individuals to operate more freely and with fewer requirements. The rationale for this relief is that so-called "accredited investors" and similar privileged categories have sufficient knowledge, assets, and sophistication to use the markets in a prudent and responsible way; imposing rules intended for novitiates or for the naive is simply unnecessary. Within the last few years, however, the CFTC has moved steadily in that same direction.

This trend in regulatory policy is highly significant in the derivatives field where institutions dominate trading and where, as a result, there are relatively few regulatory requirements. The one exception, noted earlier, is in the area of exchange-traded derivatives where anyone, regardless of size or sophistication, is welcome and, accordingly, a "one size fits all" regulatory attitude makes sense. But the over-the-counter derivatives markets, which are confined mainly to institutions, are virtually unregulated.

Does this policy make sense? Should some of our most important enterprises like banks, pension plans, and insurance companies be exempted from governmental oversight in their derivatives dealings? Even if they meet our expectations for knowledge and sophistication, a misstep by one of these giants could ripple through the entire economy and create a major crisis. Failure of a major bank could bring down other banks, which, in turn, could cripple the business community and lead to economic chaos. Known as a "systemic effect," this domino reaction should be worrisome to any regulator, even if the odds are against it ever happening. The near collapse of Long-Term Capital Management in the fall of 1998, despite its acknowledged sophistication and trading acumen, and the $3.6 billion bailout engineered by Wall Street, has everyone wondering about the institutional exceptions from most regulatory programs.

It is also true that many "institutions" get that way by amassing the savings of tens of thousands of families. This is true of banks and pension plans, for instance. Were the proposition put to regulators that families do not require protections, it would be rejected out of hand. Why, then, should less protection be provided to institutions where those savings have been centralized? Just as derivatives dealers learned in the Orange County bankruptcy that they were now dealing, not with bureaucrats, but with furious taxpayers, a catastrophe in one of these institutions that inflicts suffering on small depositors or pensioners could force the regulators to rethink their distinctions on this subject. As a result, the future legal trends in the derivatives world will be guided as much by events as by dispassionate policy.

CHAPTER 4

Where the Risks Are

Markets go up; markets go down. There is nothing insightful or sage about that observation. Derivatives, like any other market positions, are subject to this *market risk*. But while a normal investment may glide along a geometric path in response to changing market conditions, derivatives may have special features that create erratic behavior or that accelerate or exaggerate the results. For instance, an interest rate swap where the parties agree to pay each other *20 times* any change in the reference rate can cause losses to mount at an alarming rate. Or a derivative that has an odd duration or unusual characteristics may react to market developments differently from a mainstream product. In this chapter, the existence of fundamental market risk is taken for granted. More attention is paid to other risks, some of which may not come easily to mind.

VALUATION RISK

Except for exchange-listed derivatives (and even there, if the markets are thinly traded), it can be extremely difficult to assign a reliable value to derivatives where they may be very customized or where an objective and accurate price reporting system does not exist. In complex derivatives, valuation may require analysis of the instrument's various internal components, some of which may react favorably to market developments while others may sustain losses at the same time. In these circumstances, the basic question "Am I winning or losing?" may be hard to answer. On a number of occasions, end users of derivatives have complained (even in court) that their trusted dealers left them in the dark about what was happening to their positions until massive losses occurred.

Even aside from trying to place a current value on a derivatives position, it can be difficult to assess whether the fee charged on the transaction by the promoter or dealer is fair and competitive. There is no table in the *Wall Street Journal* to consult, and even if other fee structures can be identified, they may not be for the exact type of transaction that you are contemplating. One trustee of a massive pension plan told me that he does not use O-T-C derivatives because he cannot conduct "due diligence" on the fairness of the fees being charged.

TIMING RISK

Everyone would prefer to learn of bad news as soon as possible, before things get worse. Aside from the *details* of the problem, the speed with which it is detected is a critical part of risk management. As a result, users of derivatives need to be aware that losses may not be recognized as quickly as one might wish, depending on whether trading is occurring on an organized exchange or in the O-T-C market.

The formal derivatives markets where futures contracts and many options are traded have a long history of aversion to credit risk, while, at the same time, they maintain an "open door" policy toward participation by the general public. To reconcile these seemingly incompatible policies, the markets use certain devices that are calculated to avoid defaults or, failing that, to confine the damage. The mechanisms used for this purpose include the following:

Margins   Exchanges set minimum margins (deposits) that traders must maintain in their accounts. At the beginning, a trader is required to deposit an "initial" margin amount with the broker, even though no losses have yet been incurred (indeed, the trader does not "own" anything yet, either). That initial margin is used to cover subsequent losses in the account, but when it has been depleted to a certain level, the broker is obliged to demand a "maintenance" margin to top off the account again. Rest assured that the broker will do just that; exchange rules hold *it* financially responsible for any unpaid trader losses.

"Trickle-Up" Liability   As just noted, the broker carrying accounts for traders is financially responsible if any of its customers defaults on payment of market losses. By federal law and exchange rules, these brokers are required to maintain substantial resources ("capital") in part because of this residual financial liability. Consequently, when one does business on an organized exchange, there is comfort in the fact that a well-capitalized broker is standing behind every trade.

Clearing   Federal regulators have insisted that the organized exchanges must utilize a "clearinghouse" not only to sort out each day's trading and to maintain complete trading records, but to *guarantee* the financial obligations in the market. As a rule, this is done by a pooling of resources by certain (generally large) exchange member firms acting as "clearing members" with which every broker is obliged to maintain a relationship. Thus, in the unlikely event of a cascading default (by the trader, by the broker, and by the carrying clearing member), the funds held in the clearinghouse can become available to satisfy the deficiency.

Mark-to-Market   So far, these exchange-based safeguards have related essentially to where the funds will come from. But an equally important issue is *when* that will happen. The organized markets generally require that all market losses must be calculated and paid on a *daily basis*. Since it is often impractical for every trader to respond that fast, the broker uses its own funds to "even up" all of its accounts each day, issuing margin calls to the traders for reimbursement. And it is a federal requirement that one trader's excess funds cannot be used to cover another trader's losses. If a trader does not answer a margin call promptly, the broker has a legal right to liquidate open positions in the account and will not hesitate to do so (since further losses could be its own). This system is intended to confine the actual financial exposure on a default to about one day's market movement.

In contrast to the exchanges' programs of margining, pass-through liability, clearing, and daily mark-to-market, the O-T-C dealers may not provide these safeguards. The O-T-C equivalent to margin, usually called "collateral," may actually be waived if the parties have confidence in each other's credit standing, or may not be required unless losses build to a specified amount. Even where collateral is sought, it may not arrive on a next-day basis, as in the organized markets. And at this writing, there is no mutualized risk-sharing program like clearing in the O-T-C world. Thus, on O-T-C derivative transactions, losses may be allowed to accumulate for extended periods of time. Not only does this increase the risk of an eventual default, but it can make the parties somewhat complacent about keeping track of their holdings on a diligent basis. Add, further, the difficulty noted earlier in doing valuations of many O-T-C derivatives, and that risk can be further exacerbated.

CREDIT RISK

Many derivatives transactions are premised on a belief that, regardless of what happens, the counterparty will be able to pay up. While deposit of collateral frequently occurs, most derivatives users prefer not to commit precious capital in this manner and try to confine business to counterparties where collateral can be waived. But bad things happen, and even the most attractive counterparty on the transaction date can become a credit calamity later on.

A number of events can occur that starkly change the credit picture. Most obvious is a business setback at the counterparty. Probably as likely is a failure among that counterparty's suppliers or customers, or its lenders or borrowers, that cripples the counterparty as well. Accordingly, a meaningful credit assessment means more than examining the other side's balance sheet and profit-and-loss statement; a review of its exposure to third parties is critical.

And credit risk cannot always be assessed by simply tracking one's own dealings with a counterparty. In many cases—hedge funds are a good example—a portfolio of investments and derivatives may be built on loans and other credits extended by a dozen or more banks. Reports concerning the deterioration of Long-Term Capital Management in the fall of 1998 emphasized that loans had allowed it to hold assets 20 times or more greater than its own capital, much of which had been provided by banks that were unaware of Long-Term's overall debt obligations.

It is also important to understand what recourse you have if a default occurs. Your lawyers enter at this point. If the counterparty becomes insolvent and seeks legal protection under the bankruptcy laws or similar shelters, what are your chances of recovering any of your losses? At one time, a trustee in bankruptcy could look over your counterparty's entire portfolio of O-T-C derivatives, disavow those with losses, and keep those that were profitable. This practice of "cherrypicking" is no longer possible in the U.S. and in many other jurisdictions, but remains available in some countries. Similarly, until recently it might have been necessary, despite your counterparty's bankruptcy, to continue to make payments on derivatives that were profitable to the bankrupt, while having to pursue its payments owed to you in lengthy court proceedings (with no assurance of success). That dilemma has also been largely solved in the U.S. where you would be allowed to "net" across all of the derivatives with the counterparty and to pay only the remaining amount, if any. But, again, netting may not be available in some other countries.

LEGAL RISK

In a way, the bankruptcy scenario just discussed is a legal risk as well. And running afoul of the regulatory requirements discussed in Chapter 3 is a legal matter, too. But it is necessary to consider less obvious legal risks. One is that your counterparty is not *authorized* to enter into a derivatives transaction with you. Perhaps its corporate charter, or the local laws governing its operations, or some other form of legal inhibition, forbids it from engaging in this activity. Lawyers call it *ultra vires*, and it can be an excuse to renege on obligations later. In England, for example, the London boroughs of Hammersmith and Fulham avoided paying derivatives losses by claiming successfully that they were never authorized to deal in such instruments.

Derivatives, as discussed in Chapter 1, are make-believe activities using real money. No *real* dealing in the benchmarked thing occurs. Rather, the parties simply tote up their profits or losses depending on what happens in the real world. One might uncharitably compare derivatives to "bets," and, alas, there is another legal risk.

Great care must be taken to assure that the legal climate where the parties (both of them) operate recognizes derivatives as legitimate rather than as gambling devices. If they are vulnerable to being treated as gaming, the transactions may not be enforceable and the losing party may escape its obligations entirely. Indeed, because gambling is a "public policy" (not to mention a *criminal*) matter, the state may prohibit the parties from honoring their obligations even if they want to!

OPERATIONAL RISK

As noted before in this book, "tracking" one's derivatives holdings can be quite difficult since, at least in the case of O-T-C derivatives, there may be no real market for them and no price reporting service, so that the necessary mechanisms for measuring and valuating the derivatives portfolio must often be maintained internally. A number of vendors exist who sell software designed to help, including measuring volatility and performing "stress tests" against various risk scenarios, but the fact that large losses continue to occur in the derivatives arena suggests that the perfect program has yet to be developed.

A large number of well-meaning end users of derivatives, recognizing the operational demands imposed by participating in this activity, have designed elaborate "risk management" policies and procedures. The documentation for these programs can consume hundreds of pages, and to the naked eye, it is a very impressive sight. They typically create special committees to oversee the derivatives activity and define what units are to get what reports of that activity. The resulting complex organizational structure frequently results in a large schematic at the end of the document, complete with arrows and paths and dots and boxes, intended to summarize the preceding prose, which, because of its length or tedious nature, has failed to penetrate the reader's brain.

While it is imperative that any user of derivatives must develop a risk management program, the tendency must be resisted to create a complex system of checks and balances no matter how good it looks on paper. As is true in every area of successful management, *who* is involved means far more than the structure of the system itself. I have seen elaborate derivatives risk management policy statements that involve dozens or scores of people, but each of them has only a slice of the responsibility of making the program work. When I ask the obvious question "Who's in charge?" no one seems to know. And so if this book leaves with you no other thought, please remember that *your derivatives risk management system will not work unless somebody's career is at stake, and it will work best if that "someone" is in senior management with a shot at the top job, stock options, perks, and other emoluments of high office in jeopardy.* I appreciate that this is hardball, but consider what you are dealing with.

Finally, let us pay tribute to Nick Leeson. He was the futures trader in Baring's Bank (Singapore) whose activities brought about that venerable institution's collapse. The sad truth is that "rogue traders" exist and that there is no perfect defense against them. Even very well managed organizations can be victimized in this way, though they can take steps to reduce the odds. The initial hiring process can look for a past history of erratic behavior, or of unnerving derring-do, or similar hints of instability. But most rogue traders become such on the *current* job, and so it is perhaps more useful to examine what exists within the organization's *own environment* that could breed these culprits.

Three factors need to be considered. First, derivatives are a fairly new phenomenon in most organizations. The derivatives trader's place in the grand order of things may not yet be clear. He or she may not fit neatly under the wing of any part of the top management, a sort of orphan on the organizational chart. Maybe being in sales, or in planning, is seen as a "fast-track" position, but the derivatives trader's status is likely to be murky at first. One way to break out of that fog, however, is to make buckets of money for the company, and that means taking huge risks. More than a few rogue traders became that way in order to impress the boss, there being no other way evidently available to gain respect for the job. And so every end user of derivatives should take steps to make the derivatives trader feel welcome and valued without direct regard to the bottom line.

Second, too frequently the derivatives trader is "supervised" by someone who stands to gain from the trading that is conducted. Bonuses, or even promotions, may await those under whose watch a lot of trading profits were made. In this environment, it defies human nature to think that the supervisor will discourage risk taking by the derivatives trader. Even under the best of circumstances, the supervisor is likely to impose controls far later than if he or she had no economic stake in the trading program. Therefore, a strong risk management program requires that effective supervision must be conducted by persons who do not have this conflict of interest.

Finally, rogue traders can emerge in otherwise fine organizations if the risk policy is not uniformly enforced. Trading outside the parameters set by the company will not always generate losses; it can also produce huge profits. In that event, the organization may be tempted to look the other way, or to simply give the trader a mild rebuke. What the trader understands from this experience is that the company is not *really* serious about controlling its risks. In time, other breaches of the trading restrictions will happen, eventually with potentially catastrophic consequences. A meaningful risk management program will impose the same discipline on a rogue trader regardless of whether the violation generates profits or losses.

ACCOUNTING RISK

The author is not an accountant, but it is clear from news stories that the way in which derivatives transactions are accounted for in financial statements is and probably will remain the subject of great debate in the United States. In part, this is because so many derivatives transactions are *related* to other business being conducted (e.g., to hedge against price risks). As a result, reporting the outcome of one "side" but not the other could be very confusing to investors and financial analysts. This may not be a problem when both the derivatives results and the related business outcome occur simultaneously, but there is often a gap when one or the other is realized first.

Suppose, for instance, that the derivatives trade is made to protect against a rise in the price of a needed raw material. Suppose further, as luck would have it, that price actually declines dramatically so that large savings will be realized when the raw material is actually acquired but, at the same time, the derivatives transaction could suffer largely offsetting losses. In the event that the derivatives transaction is closed out before the materials purchase takes place, it will look like something very bad has happened. Conversely, if the materials purchase predates the closing out of the derivatives position, the true gain will be substantially overstated for a time.

The Financial Accounting Standards Board announced on June 1, 1998, that it has resolved unanimously to begin requiring that derivatives be reflected as assets or liabilities on the financial statements of users and that they be carried on the balance sheet at fair value as either assets or liabilities. Certain special treatment will be given to derivatives that constitute *bona fide* hedges of other exposures. The new rules were published in mid-June 1998 as *Statement of Financial Accounting Standards No. 133: Accounting for Derivative Instruments and Hedging Activities.*

This outcome was vigorously opposed by a number of interests, even to the point of urging that FASB be excluded and that the government make the decision instead. Noting that opposition, the FASB stated:

> But the Board firmly believes in the public's right to know and understand the companies in which they invest. Derivatives are complex financial instruments that can be an effective risk management tool. However, as we have learned from several well-publicized incidents, they can also expose the institution or company that trades in derivatives to potential ruin. Unfortunately, the millions of Americans who are faced with investment decisions for their retirement, the down payment on their first home, or their children's education have no way to know if a company may be in precarious financial condition. That's because derivatives generally did not need to be accounted for in financial statements.

The bitterness of the preceding debate bled through the announcement as FASB's chairman cited the need to "avoid placing the interests of any particular group over the consumers' interests" and the "self-serving objective of special interest groups," as well as "some who would like to diminish the FASB by putting standard setting smack in the hands of the federal government" which would lead to political interference in the standard-setting process. Thus, citing the All-American icons of a safe retirement, home ownership, and education, FASB delivered the "bad" news that derivatives could no longer be ignored on the balance sheet of an institution or company.

The wounds will not heal quickly, and further efforts to reverse the FASB decision cannot be dismissed. In this environment, a degree of "accounting risk" will continue to exist.

Outside the U.S., accounting standards are far from uniform. This creates the possibility that each of the parties to a derivatives transaction may carry it on the books in a different way but in conformity with local practice. Even derivatives transactions between affiliates of a multinational organization located in different countries run the risk of being booked differently unless uniform management controls can be put in place that do not violate national accounting norms. The FASB announcement discussed earlier made reference to international accounting risk:

> The United States is home to the broadest, deepest, and most liquid capital markets in the world, [FASB Chairman] Jenkins noted. "No small part of the reason is because we have the best financial reporting in the world. The transparency and completeness of our financial reporting cannot be compared to any other country. Contrast US reporting to countries like Thailand and Indonesia, whose markets are in turmoil right now. Part of their trouble stems from the fact that investors are wary that companies are withholding information about losses; losses that can be easily hidden under those countries' accounting and reporting systems."

BOUNDARY RISK

While derivatives regulators worldwide are meeting routinely in an effort to harmonize their laws and policies, a single regulatory regime is still a distant dream. Reference has already been made to differences that can exist across borders on matters like bankruptcy, gambling laws, and accounting standards. But some of the most critical distinctions may not even be noticed until a crisis forces them to the surface.

When the Baring's Bank collapse occurred, regulators in the United States, Japan, the United Kingdom, and Singapore shifted into high gear. Baring's sustained its crippling losses in the Singapore and Tokyo markets. It was headquartered in the U.K. And it had substantial interests in the U.S. that could be threatened as well. Until that time, there had been a generalized assumption among the regulators in Singapore, the U.K., and the U.S. that their laws offered similar protections to innocent customers in these circumstances (Japan did not have these particular safeguards on its affected markets). That protection consisted of a form of "customer-funds segregation" designed to remove those funds from the general accounts of the broker, to prevent their use except to finance the customers' own trading, and to permit easy identification of what belonged to customers if a crisis were to arise.

As the regulators struggled to contain the damage of the Baring's collapse, however, it became clear that the "segregation" programs even among Singapore, the U.K., and the U.S. were markedly different in actual practice. In the United States, "customers" meant anyone not affiliated with the broker, and all customers' funds were required to be kept in a special separate bank account. In the U.K., however, certain customers (principally the larger institutions) were allowed to "opt out" of its segregation plan and to commingle their funds with the broker's. As a result, it became necessary to delve into the broker's own account and try to remove the institutions' money, a lengthy process. Finally, the Singapore system of segregation allowed a broker's own affiliates to be treated as customers and to place their funds in the special account. It took considerable time for regulators to separate the affiliates' money from those of true customers. What had seemed to be the same simply was not.

The legal climate in various countries may also affect their response time in crises. In a litigious nation like the United States, any rescue plan will be reviewed carefully because of the risk that (1) it will be cited in lawsuits as a tacit admission of liability and (2) it will become a "precedent" effectively obligating a similar response in all future crises. These concerns were at work in New York when a clearing member firm of Commodity Exchange, Inc., suffered bankruptcy. While the exchange might have met the shortfall to customers of several million dollars with a simple loan from the banks, the considerations just discussed caused it to abandon that choice. By comparison, when the Baring's Bank failed in the less litigious Singapore, the local Singapore International Monetary Exchange promptly supplied the funds necessary to make whole all of the customers, in the expectation of eventually retrieving its contribution from culpable parties.

Each of the risks identified so far essentially blames someone else (the lawyers, accountants, rogues, etc.) for derivatives perils. But there are other factors at work that may be surprising, and many of them are self-inflicted. The rest of this chapter will examine a few of them.

POLLYANNA RISK

A confidence bordering on arrogance can sometimes be found in the derivatives business. Nowhere is this more manifest than in the attitude toward regulation of any kind. Either it is declared to be totally unnecessary, or it should be imposed only on competitors. We are told that dealers and users of derivatives are simply so shrewd, so well trained, and so well capitalized that regulation is a profligate waste of taxpayers' money. In the one area of derivatives activity where major regulation takes place—the exchange-listed variety—even those markets sound the same theme for their institutional clientele in a desperate effort to "level the playing field" with the O-T-C derivatives community.

Some very large derivatives losses have been sustained by major financial and commercial enterprises, which also seem to be breeding grounds for rogue traders. It would be difficult to argue that less risk is taken, but some claim that the damage sustained from those risks is somehow better contained by the institutional character of the participants. Within limits, of course, this position is unassailable. But it is all a matter of size; a truly catastrophic loss (as with Baring's) can destroy even the grandest edifices, and, worse, the potential collateral damage to the financial markets and the broader economy is clearly more acute in the case of an institutional collapse. Accordingly, the stakes are very high and it would behoove every manager to remember that even Masters of the Universe can produce bad toys.

"FORREST GUMP" RISK

It is frequently assumed that because most derivatives dealings are between corporations and institutions, neither party (nor any intermediating dealer) can credibly claim to have been overreached by the other side. After all, each of them has the resources to examine the transaction from a variety of angles, to measure the probable risk, and otherwise to make a fully informed and mature decision. And during the courting game leading up to the transaction, each party may take pains to convey the image of a knowledgeable, sophisticated participant who is wise to the world of derivatives.

This assumption can be sorely tested, however, when one of the parties experiences painful losses. In that case, it may become very "slow," professing to have not understood what was being proposed to it, or claiming to have been the recipient of only selective information from the counterparty (or a dealer). It may try to portray the other party (or a dealer) as a trusted "adviser" who owed it a legal duty to explain more or even to recommend against what in hindsight was a dangerous gamble. Gibson Greetings prevailed on just such a theory, and it will not be the last.

Overcoming the risk that a counterparty will metamorphose into a victim is not easy. Following Gibson Greetings, counsel for some of the dealers urged them to include in any transaction papers an explicit disclaimer of being the other side's adviser. This strategy caused a public relations backlash and resulted in the end users of derivatives forming their own trade group, simply exacerbating what had already become a hostile "them-or-us" atmosphere between the dealers and the end users, their own customers. Accordingly, participants in derivatives activities should take relatively *little* comfort in the size or apparent sophistication of their counterparties.

PRETTY-FACE RISK

Somewhat akin to the Forrest Gump risk is the tendency to view a counterparty to a derivatives transaction as it appears structurally, without considering what lies beneath the surface. Very few entities meet the "institutional" test better than the pension plan of a Fortune 500 company, and the billions of dollars under the trustee's management may further reinforce that impression. Similarly, a state or local government would rarely fail to pass the "institutional" test.

Under stress, however, these types of organizations decompose into their constituent parts. The pension fund becomes an angry, politically active army of retirees. And the government dissolves into a legion of furious taxpayers. Any hope of a gentlemanly resolution of the matter is lost, and months or years of public scandal and recrimination may be in store. Every participant in the derivatives market that sees an "institution" on the opposite side, therefore, needs to ask: "Who is *really* taking my counterparty's risk?" Then, and only then, should the decision be made whether to complete the trade.

OVERHARVESTING RISK

While the general public has always been welcome in the exchange-listed derivatives world, where mechanisms like a clearinghouse offer credit protection and pervasive regulation helps the little guy get a fair shake, the O-T-C derivatives markets traditionally have been confined to larger organizations with sound credit and extensive internal management resources. Credit risk is a genuine concern that has encouraged users and dealers to choose carefully their next derivatives partners. And the complexity, or, at a minimum, the tailor-made nature of many O-T-C derivatives, tends further to restrict participation to a narrowly defined segment of the economy.

At first, in the early and mid-1980s, it would be quite rare to see an O-T-C derivatives transaction that did not involve Fortune 500 firms or top-tier financial institutions. Indeed, a number of commercial and investment banks even formed AAA-rated subsidiaries to handle derivatives in order to burnish their credit standing (and dominate the flow of derivatives business). As the popularity of O-T-C derivatives grew, the larger institutions increased their levels of participation and new, somewhat smaller organizations began to take an interest as well.

With this growth, the O-T-C derivatives dealers—those who promote and arrange transactions for end users and, not infrequently, step into the middle ("intermediate") as counterparty to each side when its own credit rating is desired by the ultimate parties—hired substantial new staff to service this business and also to expand it farther. For a time, there remained a large pool of potential derivatives users with the right credit profile and sophistication for the new hires to solicit, but, inevitably, the pickings at that level of quality became thin.

What followed was a chain of events that every manager can appreciate, and fear. The new salespeople at the O-T-C derivatives dealers, being all too aware that their jobs depended on landing more and more business, looked lower and lower into the business world for customers. It was nearly impossible to know where to stop; after all, candidates with questionable credit could always be asked to deposit collateral on their trades. Almost *any* organization might be declared as qualified for this risky business, and as the sales force mushroomed in the 1990s, most were (a practice known as "bottom fishing"). This frenzy has abated somewhat as the

O-T-C derivatives business has matured, but not until a few casualties, like tiny Odessa College in Texas, were suffered. Accordingly, both dealers and end users need to make their own cold, hard assessment about who is genuinely right for derivatives activity; the salespeople will always rationalize a justification.

The desperate search for new business by derivatives dealers is not always driven by expansion ambitions. Occasionally a very lucrative segment of their market dries up, leaving many salespeople in search of something—*anything*—to pick up the slack. Consider, for example, what the upcoming common European currency—the Euro—will do to the foreign currency markets as many distinct national currencies disappear. Currency derivatives, and especially currency swaps and options, are a significant part of the overall derivatives business. An analysis of this phenomenon by the *Financial Times* included an estimate from J.P. Morgan, a key derivatives dealer, that the Euro will cause 15 percent of its derivatives revenues to evaporate. Thus, even a derivatives firm wanting to stand still must sometimes fight to do so, and the impulse to relax counterparty standards can be intense under these circumstances as well.

SIDE-OF-THE-ANGELS RISK

As discussed in Chapter 3, the level of governmental and private regulation differs radically between exchange-listed derivatives and those available in the O-T-C markets. Whether or not such a disparity is warranted can be debated endlessly, but its reality cannot be ignored. With regard to exchange-listed futures and options, the regulatory structure involves not only the CFTC at the federal level but the national self-regulator, the National Futures Association, and each of the exchanges whose elaborate rule books bristle with mandates and prohibitions as well. On the O-T-C side, however, such regulation as exists is subtle and largely indirect, a sidebar, for example, to a bank examiner's review of a bank's overall performance.

This distinction is important not only to lawyers practicing in the field but to the business executive, too. In the highly regulated exchange-listed derivatives environment, certain safeguards are built into the system. Your money will be safeguarded against misuse; your broker will have to maintain a strong capital base; high standards of conduct are set; and remedies are spelled out. Simply by using those markets, a bundle of rights comes automatically into existence. And in a meritorious controversy, the victim will have allies in the form of the federal regulator and all interested industry self-regulators.

In contrast, the rules when dealing in the O-T-C derivatives markets are murky and, for the most part, depend on what the parties agree to. The adage "It's not what you deserve that counts; it's what you negotiate" holds true in this environment, although, of course, general laws will offer some protection against blatant fraud and other chicanery. It is not surprising, therefore, that a major focal point of the work done by O-T-C derivatives trade groups like the International Swaps & Derivatives Association is on *documentation* of O-T-C derivatives transactions. There exist standardized forms of master agreements, booklets containing uniform definitions of terms, and other aids in writing up an O-T-C derivatives trade designed to minimize any misunderstandings between the parties. These documents cover more than simply the subject matter of the transaction; they specify when a breach or default can be declared and what consequences can flow from such a declaration.

Dealers and, in particular, end users need to be alert to the fact that they are not enveloped in a blanket of preconceived protections when they operate in the O-T-C derivatives area. Anyone who suggests that the O-T-C environment is as "protected" as the regulated exchange-listed derivatives world is mistaken, except to the extent that the terms of transactions as negotiated between the parties choose to incorporate those features. This is why so much time and attention is and must be paid to what the deal *says*.

LEGAL DOUBLE-TALK RISK

As noted in Chapter 3, the legal climate for derivatives is somewhat in flux today. It is not entirely clear where a particular transaction should be placed in the pantheon of what is and what is not regulated. This ambiguity not only annoys lawyers; it can produce bizarre results in the regulatory arena as well. Let the following example be a warning:

Several years ago, an end user of swaps sustained large losses and complained that it had been misled by a major invest-

ment bank acting as dealer on the trades. Recall from Chapter 3
that the CFTC has never held that a "swap" is a futures contract,
the latter being within its own regulatory jurisdiction. Nevertheless, the CFTC filed an action against the dealer alleging that it
had violated an antifraud rule applicable only to "commodity
trading advisors" which the CFTC licenses and regulates. The
quoted term is defined to include persons who give market or
trading advice with respect to *products that the CFTC regulates.* But
this case involved swaps!

The case was settled when the dealer agreed to pay millions of
dollars in fines to the CFTC, so it will never be known whether the
CFTC was correct in suing the dealer. What is noteworthy, however,
is that the CFTC, even as it accepted the dealer's large check, insisted that it was not declaring that swaps are futures contracts or
any other instrument under its regulatory jurisdiction. This is why,
at the present time, a lawyer is hesitant to assure a client that it will
not be sued by some regulator for activity that seems remote from
that agency's responsibilities, and why dealers and end users alike
should factor this risk into their O-T-C derivatives dealings.

RATINGS RISK

Derivatives dealers in particular, but also active end users, may
readily recognize the market risks that their activities entail. They
may also be aware of a number of the other risks covered by this
book. But a tendency exists to view derivatives transactions in isolation from the overall well-being of the institution. The potential
spillover effects, however, may not be so easily contained.

Not long ago, a *Wall Street Journal* article reported that the major credit rating services (e.g., Moody's and Standard & Poor's)
were reviewing a number of major derivatives dealers with a view
toward *downgrading* their ratings due to a heavy dependence on derivatives trading for their earnings. The evident concern of the rating services was that the dealers might suffer large losses because
of their derivatives market exposures, or that their earnings depended too much on trading results. The news story estimated that
if the ratings were reduced, the dealers' borrowing expense (e.g., interest costs on their commercial paper sales) could increase by as
much as $500 million per year.

Many of these dealers are multiservice organizations engaged in securities underwritings, investment banking, brokerage services, or commercial lending in addition to (and perhaps to a greater extent than) operating a trading desk in derivatives. The prospect that the latter activity might drag down the status of the organization as a whole, even in the absence of trading losses, is difficult to accept.

This risk should be even less palatable to corporate or financial end users of derivatives. While their derivatives activities are likely to be small relative to the core business operations, it is clear that the credit rating services are aware of and are interested in this activity. In the event that derivatives become more intensively used by the company, or that the derivatives markets grow highly volatile, a possibility exists that the dreaded notice that the organization's credit rating has been "put up for review" could be received. And the company's shareholders, who likely thought that they were investing in automobile production, breakfast cereals, designer clothing, or whatever, will not be happy either.

Sensitivity to risk as a corporate policy can change as well. Either existing management may grow weary of the roller coaster nature of results in high-volatility activities, or new management may force a review of risky business. So it was when the Travelers Corporation bought Salomon Brothers in the mid-1990s. Salomon ("Solly") was renowned for making huge bets on the markets that often produced enviable profits, but, on other occasions, gutted the entire firm's profit-and-loss statement. It would not be uncommon for quarterly results to fluctuate by a hundred million dollars or more. In contrast, Travelers liked a steadier, even if more boring, payoff. And so it was no surprise that within about a year of acquiring Salomon, the new management closed down its fabled bond arbitrage group as too risky for the current corporate culture. Because Travelers was seeking to amass a financial conglomerate including investments (Salomon and Smith Barney), banking (Citicorp), and insurance (its core business), it evidently concluded that earnings convulsions would be an inappropriate image for the combined institution.

CAREER RISK

Here is why you bought this book. Business failure yields victims, sacrificial and otherwise. The derivatives traders themselves are in the crosshairs, of course, but the punishment will not stop there. Next comes this question: "Who let this happen?"—asked no doubt by someone who feels safely clear of the target zone. The bloodletting may continue into the secondary and tertiary levels of management until virtually all of the "would'a, could'a, should'a" ranks have been purged. If the derivatives results are truly devastating, the hook might actually reach into the executive suites and the boardroom, as it did at UBS and BankAmerica during 1998.

By now, it is too late to save your career. The opportunity to *prevent* disaster has been lost. As a middle manager, a promising career is gone. Higher up, a chance at the top spot, a bundle of stock options, a legacy as a leader, and even a secure retirement may be sacrificed. Perhaps you will want to read this book a second time, before it is too late.

Remember, however, that prevention is not achieved by "plans" or "policies" or "guiding principles." It is the result of unflagging *enforcement* of the rules. As noted earlier, if certain activities are not allowed, punishment should be meted out even if the violation proves to be profitable for the organization. It will not do simply to condemn the maverick as a "rogue trader" after losses occur; he or she must know to a scientific certainty that this conduct, even if obscenely profitable, will never result in a promotion or even a pardon.

CHAPTER 5

A Case Study in Catastrophe—Sumitomo and the Copper Market

Recent history is replete with examples of derivatives trading gone awry. One example appears in Appendix A of this book and involves the collapse of a British icon, Baring's Bank, triggering a manhunt, investigations in at least four countries, and some very unpleasant career changes for the bank's managers. This chapter tells a similar story, but about a major business institution that survived its ordeal and had to face the music with regulators around the world. It also involved some very curious mathematics: While the company ultimately lost an estimated *$2.6 billion,* the regulators somehow calculated a "profit" of $150 million and exacted every penny of that in retribution and restitution.

BACKGROUND

Faithful readers of the financial press in the mid-1990s will remember occasional stories about "Mr. Copper," a reclusive Japanese gentleman named Yasuo Hamanaka, who joined Sumitomo Corporation in April of 1970 at its Tokyo headquarters and was assigned three years later to a group that was responsible for marketing and hedging Sumitomo's vast copper business. By 1978, he had become the head of that operation. For the next 15 years, Mr. Hamanaka appears to have gone about his business in an unremarkable way, although trading losses eventually began to accumulate. Toward the end of 1993, however, a scheme was evidently hatched to re-coup those losses, and to make fresh profits, by manipulating the price of copper on the world market. This was done in part through cornering the supplies needed to deliver on the London and New York futures markets, thus forcing those very visible prices to rise substantially.

According to regulators, the scheme reached its critical stage in October of 1995 as Mr. Hamanaka took effective control of virtually all of the known copper used by traders on the London market. Within a month, he had achieved almost 100 percent success. It was during this exercise that the press took a keen interest in Mr. Hamanaka; unfortunately his own management may not have been equally alert. It was not until May of 1996 that Sumitomo's man-agement "reassigned" Mr. Hamanaka to other duties. Eventually, he served time in a Japanese prison while Sumitomo licked its multibillion dollar wound.

PAYING THE PIPER:
THE MASSIVE CFTC SETTLEMENT

Below is the document created by the U.S. Commodity Futures Trading Commission as part of its settlement of manipulation charges against Sumitomo. The settlement included payment of $150 million by Sumitomo, including $25 million to be set aside in a special escrow fund to pay restitution to injured market partici-pants. Not only was this the largest "civil penalty" ever imposed by a U.S. regulator at that time, but it added further to the com-pany's losses that were already estimated at $2.6 billion. And it tells an unfortunately familiar story of unaccountability on the trading desk, confusion within higher management, and an "in-denial" attitude by supervisors even long after the debacle has been fully bared.

Sumitomo's troubles over the copper market would not end at the regulators' door, however. A number of lawsuits were filed by traders on the other side of the market who claimed to have suf-fered large losses through Mr. Hamanaka's antics. Some of them re-main pending at this writing, but, already, Sumitomo has under-taken to pay an additional $99 million to settle six class-action (multiple plaintiffs) cases in the New York courts while continuing

UNITED STATES OF AMERICA

Before the

COMMODITY FUTURES TRADING COMMISSION

_____

                              :

In the Matter of   :   CFTC Docket No. 98-14

                              :

SUMITOMO CORPORATION,   :   ORDER INSTITUTING

                              :   PROCEEDINGS PURSUANT

                                   TO

            Respondent.   :   SECTIONS 6(c) AND 6(d)

                              :   OF THE COMMODITY

EXCHANGE

:   ACT AND FINDINGS AND

:   ORDER IMPOSING

_____   :   REMEDIAL SANCTIONS

1. The Commodity Futures Trading Commission ("Commission") has reason to believe that Sumitomo Corporation ("Sumitomo"), through the acts of one or more of its employees and agents, has violated Sections 6(c), 6(d) and 9(a) (2) of the Commodity Exchange Act, as amended ("Act"). Therefore, the Commission deems it appropriate and in the public interest that public administrative proceedings be, and they hereby are, instituted in order to determine whether Sumitomo engaged in the violations set forth herein and to determine whether any order should be issued imposing remedial sanctions.

2. In anticipation of the institution of these administrative proceedings, Sumitomo has submitted an Offer of Settlement ("Offer") which the Commission has determined to accept. Without admitting or denying the findings herein, Sumitomo acknowledges service of this Order Instituting Proceedings Pursuant to Sections 6(c) and 6(d) of the Commodity Exchange Act and Findings Imposing Remedial Sanctions ("Order"). Sumitomo, solely by virtue of its Offer and for purposes of settling this proceeding, before argument or adjudication of any issue of fact or law, consents to the use of the findings contained in this Order in this proceeding and in any other proceeding brought by the Commission or to which the Commission is a party. Sumitomo does not consent to the use of the Offer or this Order as the sole basis for any other proceeding brought by the Commission, or to the use of the Offer or this Order against it in any other proceeding by any other party. The findings contained in this Order are not binding on any other person or entity named as a defendant or respondent in any other proceeding.

3. The Commission finds the following:

a. SUMMARY

As described in more detail below, in the wake of accumulating large losses from speculative trading, the principal copper trader for Sumitomo engaged in a scheme, in conjunction with an entity operating in the United States, with the intent of manipulating the price of copper. In particular, during 1995 and 1996, Sumitomo, acting through its agent or agents, established and maintained large and dominating futures positions in copper metal on the London Metals Exchange ("LME").[6] In the fall of 1995, Sumitomo stood for

---

6 An LME copper futures contract calls for delivery of 25 metric tons of Grade A electrolytic copper. The LME trades separate contracts for delivery dates, referred to as "prompt" dates, for each business day out to three months in the future, and for additional dates out to 27 months.

delivery on a significant percentage of its maturing futures contracts. It thereby acquired a dominant and controlling cash and futures market position, which directly and predictably caused copper prices, including prices on the United States cash and futures markets, to reach artificially high levels. Sumitomo's agent or agents took these actions expressly for the purpose of creating artificially high absolute prices and an artificially high premium of nearby prices over futures prices. Sumitomo intentionally exploited these artificially high prices in order to profit on the liquidation of its large portfolio of futures contracts and holdings of LME warrants. Through these actions, Sumitomo manipulated upward the price of copper and copper futures in violation of Sections 6(c), 6(d) and 9(a) (2) of the Act.

Sumitomo contends that its copper trader's actions described below were unauthorized and hidden from other company officials. The Commission makes no findings with regard to those contentions. It believes that, without regard to those contentions, Sumitomo is properly found to have violated the manipulation provisions of the Act.

b. RESPONDENT

Sumitomo is a Japanese corporation with its principal place of business in Tokyo, Japan. During the relevant period, Sumitomo was engaged, among other things, in the marketing of copper cathode to customers throughout the world. As part of its business of marketing copper, Sumitomo engaged in futures and option transactions on world markets, including the Comex Division of the New York Mercantile Exchange ("Comex") and the LME, primarily for the purpose of "hedging" the price risks associated with the purchase and sale of copper. These copper marketing and trading functions were primarily carried out by the Copper Metals Section of Sumitomo's Non-Ferrous Metals Department.

c. FACTS

i. *Sumitomo's Copper Trading*

Sumitomo, which was incorporated in 1919, has, together with its historical predecessors, been involved in the marketing of copper metal for hundreds of years. During the period at issue in this matter, Sumitomo's copper metals business was conducted by the Copper Metals Section of the Non-Ferrous Metals Department. The primary business of the Copper Metals Section, or Copper Team as it was also known within Sumitomo, was supplying copper cathode to customers (primarily in Asia), such as cable fabricators and rod mills. In addition to sales to customers, the business also included the extensive use of the futures markets to hedge the price risks occasioned by the volatility of copper prices. Both the purchase and sale of physical copper and hedging with futures, known within Sumitomo as "dealing," were carried out by the Copper Metals Section.

In April 1970, Sumitomo first employed an individual who, in April 1973, was assigned to the Copper Metals Section. By 1975, that individual had become involved in the physical purchase and sale of copper and in dealing, under the overall supervision of the head of the Non-Ferrous Metals Department. In August 1987, he was made head of the Copper Team. From that time until at least his reassignment on May 8, 1996, he had primary responsibility for both the actual physical purchase and sale of copper and dealing in copper metal for Sumitomo. (This individual will be referred to throughout this Order as "Sumitomo's copper trader".)

In the period immediately prior to Sumitomo's copper trader's appointment as head of the Copper Team and in subsequent years, the Copper Team incurred significant losses. The losses were the result both of the actual physical purchase and sale of copper and also of speculative futures transactions initiated, together with another Sumitomo employee at the time, in an unsuccessful attempt to compensate for losses on the actual purchase and sale of copper.

Sumitomo's copper trader did not enter the unauthorized speculative trades in Sumitomo's normal bookkeeping system. Instead, he kept a record of the transactions in a series of personal notebooks.[7]

ii. *Sumitomo's Copper Trader's Arrangements with a U.S. Copper Merchant*

Beginning in late 1993, Sumitomo's copper trader entered into a series of agreements with a newly-formed U.S. copper merchant firm located in New York City, whereby Sumitomo agreed to purchase copper from the American firm on a monthly basis for the years 1994 through 1997. The agreements were embodied in a series of supply contracts that contained unusual minimum price and price participation provisions. Under the minimum price provision, Sumitomo was obligated to purchase copper at the higher of the market price (LME settlement price) at the time of shipment of the monthly quota or the minimum price set by Sumitomo during a specified time period. The contracts also required the U.S. copper merchant firm to pay Sumitomo, as price participation,

---

7 Sumitomo contends that this speculative futures trading was unauthorized and initiated without the knowledge or consent of the copper trader's superiors at Sumitomo. The copper trader has admitted under oath, as part of his guilty plea to criminal charges of forgery and fraud in Tokyo District Court, that he employed a wide variety of complicated trading and accounting techniques to hide the losses from Sumitomo management. He stated that he lied to his superiors, destroyed documents, falsified trading data and forged signatures.

thirty percent of any positive difference between the market price at the time of shipment and the minimum price on futures contracts established to hedge the supply contracts. Thus, as copper prices rose above the pre-established minimum price, the U.S. firm and Sumitomo would share in the price appreciation, giving both firms a financial interest in higher prices.[8]

By June 15, 1994, Sumitomo's copper trader and the U.S. copper merchant had entered into six such minimum price contracts providing for the delivery of 834,000 metric tons of copper, on a schedule of roughly 10,000 metric tons per month in 1994 and 30,000 metric tons per month in 1995 and 1996. On December 1, 1994, they entered into another, similar contract for delivery of 30,000 metric tons per month in 1997. The germs of these contracts were essentially identical and in sum called for the delivery of a total of 1,194,000 metric tons of copper from 1994 through 1997. In 1995 and 1996, these contracts were used by Sumitomo's copper trader and the U.S. copper merchant to provide a justification for Sumitomo's purported need for copper to sell to customers. However, fully half of the 1995 and 1996 contractual copper was immediately resold to the U.S. copper merchant's supplier and was never actually delivered to Sumitomo.

---

8 Sumitomo contends that the minimum price and price participation provisions were not submitted through the company's normal approval channels and were unknown to the copper trader's superiors at Sumitomo.

As early as February 1994, Sumitomo's copper trader and personnel at the U.S. copper merchant firm communicated about ways they could act in concert through market operations to cause copper prices to increase.[9]

In order to effect and synchronize their joint market operations, Sumitomo's copper trader and the U.S. copper merchant established several highly unusual accounts, called the "B" accounts, at a number of brokerage houses. Under the "B" account arrangements, Sumitomo's copper trader authorized personnel at the U.S. firm to effectuate LME futures trades and other copper business in Sumitomo's name and using Sumitomo's credit. Sumitomo's copper trader gave the U.S. copper merchant power of attorney over the trading in these "B" accounts pursuant to documentation on which he forged the signatures of his superiors. Concerted market actions between the two firms took place in the ensuing years in large part through use of the various "B" accounts.[10]

During this same period, Sumitomo's copper trader and personnel at the U.S. copper merchant were in daily communication

---

9 Sumitomo contends that these communications were intentionally hidden from the copper trader's superiors at Sumitomo.

10 As with the minimum price and price participation provisions discussed above, Sumitomo contends that its copper trader did not submit any of the "B" account documentation through the company's normal approval channels and that the trading in those accounts was unauthorized and hidden from the trader's superiors.

concerning the coordination of their market activities with a view toward increasing LME copper prices. Sumitomo's copper trader and the U.S. copper merchant agreed that they should strive, through their purchases of physical metal in LME warehouses and elsewhere as well as their purchases of futures and options contracts, to inflate artificially the market price of copper to a level that would enable Sumitomo and the U.S. copper merchant to liquidate their large futures market position and holdings of LME warrants at a substantial profit.[4]

iii. *Efforts to Manipulate Copper Prices in 1995–96*

During the summer of 1995 and through the fourth quarter of 1995, Sumitomo's copper trader and the U.S. copper merchant plotted and executed their scheme to push copper prices to an artificially high level and then exit the joint operation by liquidating their massive long futures positions and holdings of LME warrants. The focus of these efforts ultimately was the acquisition of all of the stocks of deliverable copper in LME warehouses. Sumitomo's and the U.S. copper merchant's positions and actions during this period bore little relationship to their legitimate merchandising needs, but rather were specifically designed to cause artificial prices and price relationships.

In the fall of 1995, Sumitomo's copper trader authorized the acquisition of 100% of LME warehouse stocks by Sumitomo, with the

U.S. copper merchant, and set out detailed instructions for the management of Sumitomo's large portfolio of futures positions. As Sumitomo's copper trader knew, the concentration of ownership of all, or essentially all, of the LME warehouse stocks in the hands of cooperating market participants and the withholding of such stocks from the market would have the effect of increasing the price of copper and also creating a large backwardation.[11] These developments allowed Sumitomo's copper trader to liquidate, lend or roll forward Sumitomo's large market holdings at the higher price or price differential and thereby earn significant profits for Sumitomo.

Pursuant to the plan, beginning in late October 1995, Sumitomo, through its copper trader, rapidly increased its ownership and control of LME deliverable warehouse stocks. By November 24, 1995, Sumitomo owned 93% of all LME warehouse stocks through one brokerage house alone. Combined with holdings at other brokerage houses, Sumitomo, together with the U.S. copper merchant, owned and controlled up to 100% of LME stocks (including in the LME warehouse in Long Beach, California) at various times in the fourth quarter of 1995. Sumitomo also main-

---

11 Backwardation is a market condition in which the price of the commodity for near-term delivery stands at a premium to the price of the commodity for deferred delivery.

tained large and controlling LME futures positions during the fourth quarter, which Sumitomo and personnel at the U.S. copper merchant managed in a manner that bore little legitimate relationship to the marketing of physical copper to Sumitomo's customers, but rather were specifically designed to cause artificial prices and price relationships.

At the same time, cash copper prices increased sharply as did the backwardation of cash to three-month forward prices. Once these artificial prices and price relationships were attained, Sumitomo reaped substantial profits by a combination of lending forward and outright sales of positions.

Sumitomo's dominance and control of physical stocks as well as its maintenance of large futures market positions persisted into spring 1996. Beginning with the announcement of the reassignment of Sumitomo's copper trader in May 1996, Sumitomo's market dominance began to decline. Thereafter, copper prices dropped from highs of around $2,800 per metric ton to below $2,000 per metric ton after the announcement of his dismissal. These price levels persisted for several months thereafter.

iv. *Impact on Prices and Markets in the United States*

The impact on prices and markets in the United States from Sumitomo's conduct was direct and flowed from the well-established and well-known pricing relationships that exist between the LME and the U.S. cash and futures markets. First, the trading on Comex was directly affected. This was particularly true once the LME established its warehouse in Long Beach, California. During those periods of time when the LME price was manipulated into a premium over the Comex price, stocks in the United States were drawn away from Comex-designated warehouses (principally in Arizona) to LME warehouses (principally in Long Beach, California). Most importantly, the artificial prices and backwardation of prices on the LME also caused prices on the Comex to become similarly distorted and artificial as arbitrage trading between the LME and the Comex brought Comex prices higher than they otherwise would have been. Moreover, because copper contracts are generally priced by reference to the LME price or the Comex price, Sumitomo's conduct caused distorted and artificial pricing of copper, including throughout the United States cash market.

d. VIOLATIONS OF SECTIONS 6 (c), 6 (d) AND 9 (a) (2) OF THE ACT

Sumitomo, like any company or entity, acts through its employees or other agents. In this instance, Sumitomo contends that the actions that were taken by Sumitomo's copper trader were taken without authorization or knowledge of his superiors. As noted earlier, the Commission makes no findings with regard to that contention. Nevertheless, the Commission is satisfied that pursuant to Section 2(a) (1) (A) (iii) of the Act, 7 U.S.C. § 4, the "act[s], omission[s] or failure[s]" of Sumitomo's copper trader and any other agents or employees of Sumitomo in connection with the events described in this order are properly deemed those of Sumitomo. Thus, as discussed in more detail below, in pursuing the course of action set forth above, Sumitomo attempted to manipulate and did manipulate upward the price of copper in interstate commerce and for future delivery on or subject to the rules of a contract market, in violation of Sections 6(c), 6(d) and 9(a) (2) of the Act, 7 U.S.C. § § 9, 13(b) and 13(a) (2).

> As the United States Court of Appeals for the Eighth Circuit stated, We think the test for manipulation must largely be a practical one if the purposes of the Commodity Exchange Act are to be accomplished. The methods and techniques of manipulation are limited only by the ingenuity of man. The aim must be therefore to discover whether conduct has been intentionally engaged in which has resulted in a price which does not reflect basic forces of supply and demand.

Cargill, Inc. v. Hardin, 452 F. 2d 1154, 1163 (8th Cir. 1971).

The Commission has set forth the following elements of manipulation:

(1) that the [respondent] had the ability to influence market prices;

(2) that [the respondent] specifically intended to do so;

(3) that artificial prices existed; and

(4) that the [respondent] caused an artificial price.

In re Cox, [1986–1987 Transfer Binder] Comm. Fut. L. Rep. (CCH) ¶'23,786, at 34,061 (CFTC July 15, 1987).

First, Sumitomo certainly had the ability to influence market prices. Sumitomo held massive futures positions and ultimately acquired virtually total ownership of LME warrants. Sumitomo strategically withheld these physical holdings from the marketplace until prices rose to levels that were consistent with Sumitomo's trading objectives. Copper prices rose to artificial levels to attract new supplies not already controlled by Sumitomo to satisfy Sumitomo's continued demand for copper.

Second, the Commission has long recognized that the intent to create an artificial or distorted price is the *sine qua non* of manipulation. *In the Matter of Indiana Farm Bureau Cooperative Association, Inc.,* [1982–1984 Transfer Binder] Comm. Fut. L. Rep. (CCH) ¶21,796, at 27,282 (CFTC December 17, 1982). In the words of the Fifth Circuit, "there must be a purpose to create prices not responsive to the forces of supply and demands' the conduct must be calculated to produce a price distortion." *Volkart Brothers, Inc. v. Freeman,* 311 F. 2d 52, 58 (5th Cir. 1962). Manipulation is, at bottom, "the creation of an artificial price by planned action, whether by one man or a group of men." *General Foods Corp. v. Brannan,* 170 F. 2d 220, 231 (7th Cir. 1948), cited with approval in *Indiana Farm, ¶21,796 at 27,281.*

It is clear that Sumitomo, through its agent or agents, intentionally acquired and maintained a dominant and controlling position in both the physical supply of deliverable LME warehouse stocks and in maturing LME futures positions. At various times within the period in question, Sumitomo owned virtually all deliverable LME copper stocks. These positions were not intended to meet Sumitomo's legitimate commercial needs. The intent motivating the acquisition and control of both the cash market positions and the futures market positions was expressly to create artificially high absolute prices and artificially high and distorted premium of nearby prices over futures prices. Sumitomo deliberately exploited its market dominance in order to profit when market prices became artificially high, as Sumitomo had foreseen and planned.

Third, artificial prices existed. Sharp price and backwardation increases resulted from Sumitomo's acquisition of dominant cash and futures positions which were not related to their legitimate commercial needs. As the Commission has observed, when a price is affected by a factor which is not legitimate, the resulting price is necessarily artificial. *See Indiana Farm*, ¶21,796, at 27,282 n.2.

Finally, it is clear that Sumitomo's conduct was at least a substantial cause of these artificial prices. As Sumitomo's acquisition of stocks increased, LME prices increased sharply and went into a steep backwardation which rose to over three hundred dollars. As a result, copper moved from Comex warehouses in Arizona to the LME warehouse in California. Moreover, by virtue of arbitrage trading and other factors linking the trading of copper on the Comex with that on the LME, Sumitomo's activity caused the upward manipulation of copper futures prices on the Comex. Because copper contracts are generally priced based on the LME price or the Comex price, Sumitomo's actions manipulated the prices in the cash markets, including in the United States cash market. As noted earlier, these manipulative effects on prices in interstate commerce were direct, and any knowledgeable participant in copper trading would know they would result from Sumitomo's conduct, since they flowed from the well-established and well-known pricing relationships between the LME and the U.S. markets. These effects were certainly readily foreseeable and apparent, and Sumitomo knew, through its agent or agents, that this conduct would cause injury in those markets.

Sumitomo's conduct, therefore, satisfies all of the requisite elements of the offense of price manipulation.

4. In the course of the Commission's investigation of this matter, Sumitomo's management has provided substantial cooperation to the Commission in important respects. The company fully informed and cooperated with the Commission and other international regulatory authorities, including Japanese authorities, in connection with Sumitomo's public revelation in June 1996 of its large

positions and related losses in the copper market. At the Commission staff's request, the company announced its intention to stand behind contracts that were traded by the U.S. copper merchant, and the company ultimately reported a significant cost associated with the unwinding of those contracts. The company also provided the Commission voluntarily with certain important information during the course of the investigation. It might have been difficult, if not impossible, for the Commission otherwise to obtain at least some of this information, particularly taking into account that Sumitomo is a foreign corporation.

The Commission also recognizes that the company has suffered significant losses in the wake of the collapse of the scheme underlying this action and that it faces continued exposure in private litigation. It has reported losses of $2.6 billion as a result of the matters discussed in this Order. Finally, Sumitomo's copper trader has stated that he took certain steps to hide aspects of his conduct from other company officials and the Commission notes that there have been indications that he may have personally profited from his conduct. Sumitomo has sued him in Japan for purportedly transferring millions of dollars that properly belonged to the company.

On the other hand, the conduct described above imposed enormous costs on traders, manufacturers, retailers and consumers of copper. The Commission believes that the conduct described in this Order was part of a course of conduct that extended over a much longer period of time.

Even acknowledging Sumitomo's copper trader's acts of deception, the Commission agrees with the Japanese court that stated, in the course of sentencing Sumitomo's copper trader to an eight year term of imprisonment, that Sumitomo's internal monitoring systems were inadequate, that "the company developed no effective system for controlling the action of the dealing team," and that "such system was one cause for this case." Company officials overlooked signs of the copper trader's misconduct. Various warnings from information in the marketplace and from Sumitomo's copper trader's actions of which company officials were aware provided Sumitomo with the opportunity to address Sumitomo's copper trader's actions. It did not heed those warnings or address those actions. As the Japanese court put it, "Sumitomo just considered the amount of profit that [Sumitomo's copper trader] showed, and trusted [Sumitomo's copper trader] too much, and left an insufficient monitoring system, and allowed [Sumitomo's copper trader] to be in his position for a long time, and thus it can be said that Sumitomo just sought profit too single-mindedly, and did not take care of the control for [sic] risk management. Sumitomo's responsibility is not small."

The Commission has taken all of these factors into account in its decision to accept Sumitomo's Offer of Settlement, which it believes strikes an appropriate balance among these considerations. The civil monetary penalty imposed on Sumitomo approximates the extent of Sumitomo's gains as a result of the manipulative scheme. Considering the breadth and impact of the conduct in question, that is appropriate. At the same time, the civil monetary penalty is significantly less than what the statute would provide if the matter were litigated to a successful conclusion. *See* 7 U.S.C. SS 9, 13(b) (providing for a civil monetary penalty of not more than the higher of $100,000 per violation or triple the monetary gain from the violation). The mitigating factors as well as the benefits to the Commission of resolving this matter prior to filing and the lengthy proceeding that would thereafter ensue justify this result.

5. FINDINGS OF VIOLATIONS

Based on the foregoing, the Commission finds that Sumitomo violated Sections 6 (c), 6 (d) and 9 (a) (2) of the Act, as amended, 7 U.S.C. §§ 9, 13 (b) and 13 (a) (2).

6. OFFER OF SETTLEMENT

Sumitomo has submitted an Offer of Settlement in which, without admitting or denying the allegations or the findings herein, it: acknowledges service of the Order; admits jurisdiction of the Commission with respect to the matters set forth in this Order and for any action or proceeding brought or authorized by the Commission based upon violations or for enforcement of the Order; waives service of a complaint and notice of hearing, a hearing, all post-hearing procedures, judicial review by any court, any objection to the staff's participation in the Commission's consideration of the Offer, any claim of double jeopardy based on the institution of this proceeding or the entry of any order imposing a civil monetary penalty or other relief, and all claims which it may possess under the Equal Access to Justice Act, 5 U.S.C. §504 (1994) and 28 U.S.C. §2412 (1994), as amended by Pub. L. No. 104-21, §§231-32, 110 Stat. 847, and Part 148 of the Commission's Regulations, 17 C.F.R. §§148.1 et seq., relating to, or arising from, this action; stipulates that the record basis on which this Order is entered consists solely of this Order, including the findings in this Order; and consents to the Commission's issuance of this Order, in which the Commission makes findings, including findings that Sumitomo violated §§6(c), 6(d), and 9(a)(2) of the Act, and orders that Sumitomo cease and desist from violating the provisions of the Act it has been found to have violated, that it pay a civil monetary penalty of one hundred twenty-five million dollars ($125,000,000) within twenty (20) business days of the entry of this Order, that it pay an additional twenty-five million dollars ($25,000,000) into escrow within twenty (20) business days of entry of this Order, to be paid either as restitution of damages proximately caused by virtue of the conduct underlying the violations found in the Order, in the manner set forth in this Order, or as part of the civil monetary penalty, also in the manner set forth in this Order, and that it comply with its undertakings.

7. ORDER

Accordingly, IT IS HEREBY ORDERED THAT:

1. Sumitomo shall cease and desist from violating §§ 6 (c), 6 (d) and 9 (a) (2) of the Act;

2. Sumitomo shall pay a total amount of One Hundred Fifty Million Dollars ($150,000,000USD), consisting of:

  a. One Hundred Twenty-Five Million Dollars ($125,000,000 USD) as a civil monetary penalty, pursuant to Section 6(c) of the Act, which shall be paid in accordance with the terms of paragraph 3, below; and

  b. Twenty-Five Million Dollars ($25,000,000USD), which may be used within the time limitations and in accordance with the procedures set forth in paragraph 4 below, solely to pay restitution of damages (including where characterized as damages) pursuant to Section 6(c) of the Act, determined or alleged to be proximately caused to private claimants by virtue of the conduct underlying the violations found in the Order and, for those same claimants only, by virtue of similar conduct occurring at other times prior to June 30, 1996; and after the expiration of those time limitations, any remaining part of the Twenty-Five Million Dollars ($25,000,000USD) shall become part of the civil monetary penalty pursuant to Section 6(c) of the Act, in accordance with the terms of paragraph 4, below.

3. Sumitomo shall deposit the civil monetary penalty of One Hundred Twenty-Five Million Dollars ($125,000,000USD) by electronic funds transfer to the account of the Commission at the United States Department of the Treasury within twenty (20) business days of entry of this Order. Such payment shall be made in a manner authorized by the Commission and in accordance with United States Treasury regulations and shall be accompanied by a letter that identifies Sumitomo and the name of this proceeding. A copy of the cover letter and proof of payment to the United States Treasury shall be simultaneously transmitted to the Director of the Division of Enforcement (the "Division") of the Commission (the "Director").

4. Sumitomo shall deposit the remaining Twenty-Five Million Dollars ($25,000,000USD) (together with any interest thereon, the "Escrow Funds"), within twenty (20) business days of the entry of the Order, into an escrow account (the "Escrow Account") established at Citibank, N.A. ("the Escrow Agent"), which shall serve as escrow agent over the Escrow Funds, and the law firm of Shutts & Bowen, LLP, Miami, Florida, shall serve as administrator thereof (the "Administrator") to fulfill the obliga-

tions of paragraph 4b, and they shall follow the instructions set forth below:

a. The Escrow Funds shall be invested in the CitiFunds U.S. Treasury Reserves Money Market Account, which is a fund fully backed by short-term U.S. Treasury obligations.

b. The Administrator shall take all necessary steps to enable the Escrow Funds to be a taxable "settlement fund," within the meaning of Internal Revenue Code §468B and regulations thereunder, including the filing of the elections and statements contemplated by those provisions. The Administrator shall file all necessary federal, state and local tax returns for the Escrow Funds and shall pay any appropriate taxes as a "qualified settlement fund," within the meaning of Treasury Regulations 1.468B-1, et seq., 26 C.F.R. 1.468B-1 et seq., from the Escrow Funds.

As used in this Order:

(1) a "Covered Action" is a lawsuit against Sumitomo and/or its officers, directors, employees or subsidiaries (collectively, the "Sumitomo Defendants") by one or more private claimants in the courts of the United States or of any state of the United States that seeks recovery from the Sumitomo Defendants for losses or injuries that the claimant(s) allege were caused in whole or in part by activities of the Sumitomo

Defendants or their agents during a period which includes some or all of the period from June 1, 1995 to May 31, 1996, that affected (a) the price of copper in (i) a cash market, (ii) a futures market, (iii) an options market; and/or (b) the price of any product containing copper. Without limiting the foregoing, each of the following pending actions is deemed a Covered Action for the purposes of this Offer: *(1) In re Sumitomo Copper Litigation*, 96 Civ. 4584 (MP), and *Polansky* v. *Sumitomo Corporation of America, et al.*, 97 Civ. 5372 (MP), pending in the United States District Court for the Southern District of New York; and (2) *Heliotrope General, Inc.* v. *Sumitomo Corporation, et al.*, Case No. 007011679, and *R.W. Strang Mechanical* v. *Sumitomo Corporation, et al.*, Case No. 007011680, pending in the Superior Court of the State of California for the County of San Diego (together referred to as the "Pending Class Actions").

(2) The "Effective Period" shall be the period that ends four (4) years from the date of entry of the Order, provided, however, that such period shall be tolled for a Covered Action, as defined below, during the period after a Settlement Agreement in that Covered Action has been executed and before the entry of a final, non-appealable order disapproving, overturning, setting aside or otherwise nullifying a Settlement Agreement.

(3) A "Settlement Agreement" is an agreement, including in the form of an agreed-to proposed order or stipulation, in a Covered Action that (1) resolves (or, if approved by a court, will resolve) some or all claims against one or more of the Sumitomo Defendants; and (2) if court approval of the agreement, proposed order or stipulation is required by Fed. R. Civ. P. 23(e) or any analogous state statute, provides that any amounts paid to a Covered Action Fund (as defined below) from the Escrow Account shall revert to the Escrow Account if and when a final, nonappealable judgment or order is entered disapproving, overturning, setting aside or otherwise nullifying the settlement agreement.

(4) A "Covered Action Fund" is an escrow or court-administered fund established for the benefit of the private claimants pursuant to a Settlement Agreement.

(5) A "Final Disposition" is a final, nonappealable judgment or order that finally disposes of a Covered Action with respect to one or more Sumitomo Defendants.

d. The Escrow Agent shall make, at Sumitomo's written request, a payment for the purposes specified in Section 2b, above, required to be made by Sumitomo pursuant to a Settlement Agreement or Final Disposition made or entered within the Effective Period, no later than ten (10) days after satisfaction of all of the following conditions, to the persons, entities or accounts set forth in the Settlement Agreement or Final Disposition, in an amount equal to the lesser of (i) the amount requested by Sumitomo; or (ii) the remaining Escrow Funds (after payment of all fees to the Escrow Agent and Administrator pursuant to paragraph 4h below, and taxes or reserves therefor, as specified in paragraph 4b above):

(1) the private action is a Covered Action;

(2) if the action is not one of the Pending Class Actions, a copy of the pleadings has been provided to the Escrow Agent;

(3) if the payment is pursuant to a Final Disposition, the judgment with proof of entry by the court has been provided to the Escrow Agent;

(4) if the payment is to a Covered Action Fund pursuant to a Settlement Agreement in a class action (including, but not limited to, the Pending Class Actions), the Settlement Agreement (and a copy of the relevant escrow agreement, if applicable) in connection with the Covered Action Fund has been provided to the Escrow Agent. Upon the entry of a Final Disposition in such matter, Sumitomo shall advise the Escrow Agent of the Final Disposition in such matter and shall provide a copy of such Final Disposition and proof of entry to the Escrow Agent; and

(5) the payment has been approved by the Commission as consistent with the terms of its Order, and the Commission has informed the Escrow Agent in writing of its approval.

e. Sumitomo shall submit to the Division a copy of any request to make any payment from the Escrow Funds (other than a payment pursuant to paragraph 4h) along with any supporting documentation, on or before the date Sumitomo submits such request and documentation to the Escrow Agent. Sumitomo shall provide additional information reasonably requested by the Division as needed for the Commission to determine if it should approve the payment as consistent with the terms of the Order. The Escrow Agent shall not make any requested payment until it receives the Commission's written approval. If the requested payment is consistent with the terms of the Order, the Commission shall, within thirty (30) days of the request, give its written approval to the Escrow Agent or state in writing its denial of approval and the reasons for its denial.

f. In no event shall any funds paid pursuant to the Order be paid to, directly or indirectly, any current or former officer, director or employee of Sumitomo or any other defendant in any Covered Action.

g. The Escrow Funds shall be applied only to pay damages to private claimants but shall not be applied for the payment of attorneys' fees or expenses or any other costs incurred in connection with any aspect of a Covered Action other than as provided in paragraph 4h. To the extent that the amount of the judgment or settlement of a relevant action is used as the basis of setting attorneys' fees or expenses in a Covered Action, that amount shall not include any part of the Escrow Funds. The court with jurisdiction over the Covered Action shall be expressly informed by Sumitomo of the requirements of this paragraph prior to the court's consideration of any application for attorneys' fees or expenses or payment of any other costs for which Covered Action Funds are to be used.

h. The Escrow Agent and Administrator shall be entitled to payment from the Escrow Funds for all reasonable fees and expenses in connection with establishment, maintenance and termination of the Escrow Account. Such payments shall have priority over payments to claimants pursuant to paragraph 4d, above.

i. The Escrow Agent shall provide monthly reports to the Commission and Respondent which: set forth details of the disbursement of any funds from the Escrow Account; itemize the amount of interest accrued on the account; and itemize allowable expenses paid to the Escrow Agent in connection with the account.

j. Any Escrow Funds not distributed in accordance with the terms of paragraphs 4b, 4d and 4h, above, upon the expiration of the Effective Period, and any funds refunded to the Escrow Account after the expiration of the Effective Period, shall be deemed a civil monetary penalty pursuant to §6(c) of the Act and shall be paid immediately by the Escrow Agent to the United States Treasury. Such payments shall be made in the manner described in paragraph 3, above.

k. The Escrow Account shall remain open until all of the Escrow Funds have been paid pursuant to paragraphs 4b, 4d, 4h and 4j, and, in the event that a payment has been made to a Covered Action Fund, there shall have been a Final Disposition. At such time, the Escrow Agent shall terminate the Escrow Fund and shall make a final report pursuant to paragraph 4i.

l. Insofar as any part of this paragraph 4 calls for signed and/or written notification(s), authorization(s) or communication(s), a fax transmission shall be a satisfactory means of providing such notification(s), authorization(s) or communication(s).

v. Sumitomo shall comply with the following undertakings:

a. To cooperate fully with the Commission and its staff in any investigation, civil litigation or administrative proceeding related to this proceeding, by, among other things, upon the Commission's reasonable request and subject to any legally cognizable privileges, (1) providing the Commission's staff with access, for inspection and copying, to documents within the possession, custody or control of Sumitomo or any of its subsidiaries; and (2) actively seeking the cooperation of any Sumitomo officer, director or employee for interviews, depositions or testimony. Any such request will be made upon Sumitomo's counsel, Martin London and Bruce Birenboim of the law firm of Paul, Weiss, Rifkind, Wharton and Garrison. Should Sumitomo seek to change the designated person to receive such requests, notice shall be given to the Commission of such intention 14 days before it occurs. Any person designated to receive such requests shall be located in the United States.

b. Not to take any action or make any public statement denying, directly or indirectly, any statement in this Order or creating, or tending to create, the impression that the Order is without a factual basis; provided, however, that nothing in this provision affects Sumitomo's testimonial obligations, or its right to take factual or legal positions relating to any proceeding to which the Commission is not a party. Sumitomo will undertake all steps necessary to assure that all of its agents, attorneys and employees understand and comply with this agreement.

By the Commission.

_____

Jean A. Webb

Secretary to the Commodity

Futures Trading Commission

Date: May 11, 1998

to insist that it *lost* $2.6 billion in its trading operation. Sumitomo's willingness to pay regulators and private claimants large sums of money even when it had sustained huge trading losses underscores the fact that after-the-fact payouts frequently do not mean returning money wrongfully taken but constitute real, new costs incurred to put the episode to rest.

While the Sumitomo episode illustrates what can happen when a company's internal controls are inadequate, derivatives losses are not confined to rogue traders. The General Accounting Office conducted a study in 1997 that included a review of OTC derivatives losses sustained by outsiders ("end users") that had conducted their trading with OTC derivatives dealers. While the study also included mortgage-backed securities and structured notes, the GAO was able to identify no fewer than *360* instances where end users incurred losses. At least 13 of those episodes resulted in litigation where the end users accused the dealers of sharp sales practices (the GAO's chart is Appendix B in this book). Anyone can file suit, of course, and many cases lack merit. But in many of the 13 cases cited by the GAO, multimillion dollar settlements were made by the dealers in favor of those end users. For example, the State of West Virginia obtained settlements totaling $48 million, while Procter & Gamble was forgiven a debt to the dealer of roughly $150 million. And more recently, Merrill Lynch paid $400 million to settle litigation brought by Orange County, California, after the county was bankrupted by huge losses on derivatives offered by M-L. And that will not end M-L's woes; a settlement with the Belgian government over currency options was rumored in one British publication at up to $300 million (disputed by M-L). M-L did not escape the Sumitomo debacle either. It settled a class action with investors for $18 million and may also need to make peace with the CFTC. A hundred million here . . . a hundred million there . . . after a while it begins to add up, even for the finest investment firms. The message? Your derivatives people can threaten the company by hurting outsiders as well.

Sometimes the alleged "victims" of derivatives abuses are improbable counterparties, perhaps due to the "overharvesting" proclivity of hungry derivatives salespeople, discussed in Chapter 4. Why, for example, was tiny Odessa College dabbling in mortgage derivatives (it lost $10 million)? And who talked the Shoshone

Indian tribe into that same market, where a $5 million hit was taken? But the casualties can include some unexpected institutions, too. The Belgian government, for example, played the currency options market and lost big: $1.2 billion. Orange County, California, used interest rate derivatives to rack up a $1.7 billion loss, precipitating a rare bankruptcy by a local government. And a financial institution for many of the U.S. government's elite leaders engaged in risky leveraged mortgage derivatives and learned an expensive $61 million lesson.

Out there, in numbers, are also many pension plans that are playing the derivatives markets at this moment. They are permitted to do so because of a premise that is popular today, namely, that large "institutions" have the knowledge and sophistication to handle these instruments carefully and responsibly. Maybe, but the track record of other institutions suggests otherwise. And if a major pension fund were to be decimated through derivatives trading, the suffering would be felt not in the executive suite but in the budgets of thousands of retirees. Just as there was an uproar among Orange County's taxpayers (causing Merrill Lynch to settle for over $435 million), the demise of a pension plan would set off a firestorm of public protest. The derivatives community, especially its over-the-counter sector, would not remain "unregulated" for long after that.

CHAPTER 6

The International Dimension

In Chapter 4, boundary risk was briefly discussed. But exposure to risk on derivatives transactions goes beyond the idiosyncracies of variant legal rules and practices in foreign jurisdictions. The derivatives business has become truly global in scope, and with that, both dealers and end users face the risks of miscommunication caused by language barriers, different ways of conducting business in general, and in some instances a xenophobic attitude that can impede negotiations or, following a bad trade with heavy losses, can skew the outcome in favor of the local party.

THE GLOBALIZATION PHENOMENON

As noted throughout this book, derivatives come in two broad classes: those which are listed on organized exchanges and those which are privately negotiated between two parties (possibly with the help or "intermediation" of an experienced dealer). Globalization occurred first in the exchange-traded environment. While the lion's share of such business occurred on markets in the United States for over a century, the 1980s in particular witnessed a burst of development of futures and options markets around the world. A major catalyst was the invention of futures contracts on financial instruments and, in particular, on sovereign debt (government bonds). Nearly every major country uses bonds to finance its public services, and the existence of derivatives on those bonds helped to lower funding costs and to hedge against declines in market value (rising interest rates). The U.S. markets listed spectacularly successful futures contracts on U.S. Treasury bonds, notes, and bills. With a few exceptions, however, there was little interest in the U.S. to trade the government debt of other nations. Accordingly, if a similar product were to exist at all, it would have to be developed by a homegrown institution.

Prior to 1980, there were a few foreign exchanges such as the London Metal Exchange (precious and industrial metals), the London Commodity Exchange ("soft" commodities like sugar), the Tokyo Grain Exchange, the European Options Exchange (equity and currency options), the Hong Kong Futures Exchange (gold), the Sydney Futures Exchange (wool), and the Winnipeg Grain Exchange. With the creation of financial futures contracts, however, both the governments and the banks in a number of countries saw value in developing their own futures markets in sovereign debt as well as in an array of commercial loans and bank-issued instruments. From that interest emerged dozens of new futures and options markets in all major financial centers worldwide. London created what is now the London International Financial Futures & Options Exchange (LIFFE); in France the government encouraged the formation of the Marche a Term International de France (MATIF); the Germans did the same with the Deutsche Terminbörse (DTB); Spain responded with both a fixed-income market (MEFF Renta Fija) and an equity derivatives market (MEFF Renta Variable); and other derivatives exchanges were formed in Scandinavia and in central Europe.

Across the Pacific, exchanges were developed in Japan, in Hong Kong, in Singapore, in Malaysia, and in New Zealand. The trend continues. Futures markets have also been established in Taiwan, in Korea, in the People's Republic of China, in the Philippines, and in India. At this writing there is active interest in developing derivatives exchanges in other areas of the Far East as well as in the Middle East. All told, the Futures Industry Association, which is the American trade association, reports regularly on trading activity on 43 organized futures or options exchanges situated in 24 countries, while a number of additional markets do not participate in that reporting program.

While a few of the new exchanges adopted the American-style trading system of open outcry in a trading hall, most elected to use computerized trading systems instead. The first such electronic market was the New Zealand Futures & Options Exchange (NZFOE), a creature as much of necessity as of ingenuity since the NZFOE needed to operate different trading centers in Auckland (North Island) and in Christchurch (South Island) simultaneously. Other markets chose screen dealing systems for lack of a ready-made cadre of human traders to populate and to lubricate an open outcry trading hall. This has created intense competition between the two trading methodologies. The large banks and other financial institutions that patronize most of the financial derivatives markets appear to view screen dealing systems as more cost-effective than open outcry, and because they are accustomed to electronic trading for other purposes, they have little difficulty adapting to those systems. Increasingly, the open outcry markets are coming under pressure to convert or, at a minimum, to devise ways to provide the same cost savings by other means. Thus, the 1980s' phenomenon of worldwide exchange growth spawned not merely new competition but a technological revolution as well.

With this proliferation of markets came new business opportunities for the brokerage community, the banks, and investment programs. And while the quality of regulation varied widely among the exchanges, there was at least some semblance of enforceable rights and ethical rules to act as guideposts for foreign investors. Even so, disasters did occur, perhaps best illustrated by the collapse of Baring's Bank, as reflected in Appendix A in this book.

The situation grew even dicier as O-T-C derivatives became more available around the world. Frequently, whatever regulation existed did not apply to those transactions, or the private trades simply slipped by the regulators' "radar screen." This was deemed to be a modest nuisance during the late 1980s and early 1990s when many foreign economies appeared to be booming. What could go wrong, for example, during the "Asian miracle"? It took the sobering Far East correction of 1997–1998 to supply an answer.

CULTURAL AND POLITICAL WILD CARDS

For one thing, recovering amounts owed by foreign counterparties on derivatives trades can be severely imperiled when the *country* is experiencing economic trauma. In the face of potential bank collapses, default on sovereign debt, and currency devaluation, battered counterparties may relegate derivatives debts to a very low priority even when there is every expectation of eventual payment. Indeed, during the 1998 economic crisis in Indonesia, which toppled its political leadership as well as requiring International Monetary Fund intervention, there was open discussion about whether or not Indonesian counterparties would take seriously their obligations on derivatives trades. The *Financial Times* (of June 9, 1998) reported that those obligations, which could reach $15 *billion*, were being viewed in Indonesia as less urgent than other debt and that U.S. counterparties "have been working hard to disabuse them of that idea."

When the "Asian flu" struck hard in 1997, the major derivatives dealers had booked huge amounts of business in that region. By the end of the first quarter of 1998, very substantial write-offs were being made by the major dealers. In that quarter alone, for example, *Swaps Monitor* reported from dealers' regulatory filings that the top eight U.S. commercial bank dealers had derivatives-related credit losses in Asia of $121 million, up from a mere $2 million for the year-earlier period. Multimillion dollar losses hit most of the larger dealers during the Asian crisis, amounting (as of first-quarter 1998) to $144 million at Bankers Trust, $73 million at J.P. Morgan, $37 million at Citicorp, $17 million at BankAmerica, and $12 million at Chase Manhattan. Though not yet written off, derivative transactions denominated as "nonperforming" approximated $900 million when only two of the major banks were examined. And the full brunt of Asia's economic woes was not expected to impact the U.S. until later in 1998 or early 1999.

Economic stresses can also provoke political responses that jeopardize recovery on derivatives transactions. When the Malaysian ringgit came under devaluation pressure in 1997, the prime minister accused hedge fund operators of shorting the currency in a speculative attempt to destroy its value. When a derivatives party is painted at the highest levels of government as a menace to society, the chances of recovering derivatives debts in the local courts becomes problematical. Indeed, the prudent thing to do might even be to forgive the debt in the hope that it will placate the political hostility as well.

While in the mid-to-late 1990s the idea was widely embraced by the investment community that fabulous returns could be obtained by acquiring interests in "emerging markets," that ambition was (or should have been) tempered by certain realities. First, those markets had extremely immature infrastructures, that is, insufficient liquidity or prudential controls. Second, valuation of investments was painfully difficult as generally accepted accounting principles were not uniformly applied. And as every "local" in those markets would observe, the capital driving the prices skyward was being supplied largely by *foreign investment managers* who were "copycatting" each other. Insofar as fads do not last forever, and least of all when economies stumble, the capital *retreat* can prove to be even more calamitous than the original inflow was positive. Thus, a combination of highly mobile capital and fragile economic confidence is the perfect recipe for a "boom and bust" market.

In some nations where the economic system has diverged substantially from the capitalist model, there are profoundly fundamental risks even where controlled experiments in free markets are under way. I visited the People's Republic of China in 1993 to lecture on the formation of derivatives exchanges there. Armed with extensive outlines of a regulatory structure that I would propose for use by its government, I rose to make my first presentation in Beijing to a large group of public officials. Just then, our translator leaned over to me and whispered: "You do understand, I trust, that under the Chinese system there is no concept of private property?" How, then, can you have a market? If no one owns what is being sold, and the buyer does not gain ownership either, what in the world is happening there? Later, at a dinner in Shenzhen with Chinese dignitaries, one of the hosts expressed repeatedly how much he enjoyed "his" home there (the prior quarters in Beijing had not been as spacious). Recalling my translator's admonition, I asked politely how he *knew* that he owned the home. Looking a bit puzzled, he responded: "Because the [Communist] Party says I do." The remainder of my tour in China was devoted to a discussion of the "sanctity of contract" rather than to the nuances of regulatory policies.

At this writing another drama is unfolding in Seoul and New York City, where J.P. Morgan is embroiled in litigation with South Korea's SK Securities as a result of SK's loss of an estimated $300 million on two currency derivatives sold to it by Morgan that were battered when the Thai baht and the Indonesian rupiah slumped in 1997. Morgan sued in New York to recover the debt after SK had successfully sought an injunction in Seoul to block its bank from making repayments. SK is reportedly alleging that Morgan withheld information regarding the products' investment risk and that the transactions were otherwise unfair. This controversy illustrates several principles. First, international derivatives dealing can create a duel between the countries' court systems, causing confusion and delay that favors the nonpayer in that it can persuade the creditor to settle for less than the full debt. Second, the principal catalyst for the dispute was the Asian economic crisis, a phenomenon beyond either party's control. And, third, for good measure the debtor has accused the creditor of improprieties, a very common litigation strategy. It remains to be seen whether Morgan can collect even if it wins or whether, more likely, a settlement for a discounted sum is agreed.

COORDINATING REGULATORY POLICY

While global business in derivatives has blossomed in recent years, national regulators have recognized a greater need to cooperate in cross-border investigations and crises. Most of the coordination efforts have been focused on exchange-traded derivatives and involve execution of memoranda of understanding (MOU) or similar documents in which each agency agrees to share information with, or even to conduct investigations for, a foreign regulator for law enforcement purposes. Dozens of national regulators are parties to these accords, which are generally subject to conditions. First, no information is shared if it would violate national bank secrecy or similar laws. Second, the requesting agency must disclose the purpose of the request with sufficient clarity to persuade the other regulator that the inquiry is legitimate and proper. And, third, recent MOUs have provided greater detail on when, where, and how the information-sharing process will be carried out, including what types of information should generally be transferred without reservations. Two international organizations that have been especially instrumental in advancing cooperation among national regulators are the International Organization of Securities Commissions (IOSCO) and the Federation Internationale des Bourses de Valeurs (FIBV).

IOSCO and FIBV have not been notably active, however, in regard to O-T-C derivatives. Indeed, that area of the derivatives business tends to fall outside mainstream regulatory programs in most countries, including the United States. What attention has been given to the O-T-C arena has focused on capital adequacy concerns, risk analysis methodologies, and accounting standards, all of which have provoked substantial controversy. The leading advocate for the O-T-C dealers is the International Swaps and Derivatives Association, which, although it has worked toward valuable standardization for derivatives documentation and compiles important statistical data on the business, does not purport to act in any regulatory capacity. Thus, controversy over O-T-C derivative transactions tends to be resolved in the final analysis through private litigation, some of which is described in this book.

As the Baring's Bank episode (see Appendix A) demonstrated, international derivatives activity may also require positioning staff in foreign locations where supervision is difficult to conduct. But Baring's is hardly an isolated case. The Sumitomo family of companies, the central focus of Chapter 5, had a problem in the United States grain futures markets some 23 years earlier than the discovery of Mr. Hamanaka's copper activities. That company had acquired a large "short" position in corn futures for July 1973 delivery on the Chicago Board of Trade. On the final day of trading in that contract (as of the next day, delivery of physical corn would have been required), the price per bushel of July corn rose nearly $1.20, an unprecedented amount for a single day. All eyes were on a grain cooperative from Indiana that held most of the "long" contracts at that time, placing it in a position to make an excellent profit. After investigation, the CFTC's staff charged the co-op with market manipulation, but the agency refused to find any violation for legal reasons. Even so, many observers were mystified about why Sumitomo, an astute grain trading firm, would remain in the market so long without wanting delivery of real grain and then would pay sky-high prices to get out at the very last chance to do so. Could it have been that the Sumitomo traders located in the U.S. had taken larger futures positions than Tokyo authorized and, rather than highlight that error back home by taking massive deliveries of unwanted grain, had decided to liquidate their positions and to take a large cash loss that could be blamed on "market conditions"? No evidence was presented one way or the other; we may never know if Sumitomo's staff in the U.S. lost control, but the conjecture will persist.

CHAPTER 7

Doing It Right

An inevitable part of preparing for and participating in derivatives activity is to design a system of accountability that assures a flow of all relevant information to the right people in a timely manner and to construct a procedure for dealing with decision making that is both knowledgeable and responsive to the fast-paced trading environment. In essence, do we know everything that we should? Is it reaching the people who count? When action needs to be taken, who should do it?

LIVING THE NIGHTMARE

Let us begin with the worst-case scenario. Suppose an organization is aware of the potentially beneficial uses of derivatives; indeed, there may be rumors that competitors are using derivatives to their advantage. Personnel in the company's treasurer's office, including the chief financial officer, have no background or understanding of these instruments, which, except for exchange-listed derivatives, probably did not exist when they were in college or graduate school. Nevertheless, a decision is taken to hire that capability.

Enter "the trader." A first interview reveals a young, brash, and hugely self-confident individual who, whatever it is he is saying, clearly knows more about derivatives than any of the listeners. A job offer is made, perhaps with a charter to hire more traders when activity picks up. Before long, the derivatives operation has grown to include several traders, researchers, chartists, and support staff, all of them fiercely loyal to the head trader. They call themselves "us"; the rest of the company is known as "them."

The company, recognizing vaguely that derivatives trading is risky, produces an 85-page "manual" setting forth a variety of policies and procedures and identifying a score of company officials who would be somewhere in the chain of command. These would include personnel in marketing, accounting, finance, and other areas of the firm. But no one is placed directly in charge.

Operating free and clear of pesky supervision, the derivatives "desk" aspires to generate the same massive profits sometimes enjoyed at Salomon Smith Barney or Goldman Sachs or Morgan Stanley. These traders, like their colleagues everywhere, seek to achieve legendary status among their peers. They begin to load up on permitted derivatives transactions in order to supercharge the portfolio, or they ask to broaden the range of derivatives that they can trade. Management, remaining clueless, agrees.

Controlling both the trading and the flow of trade-related information to management, the derivatives desk finds it relatively easy to obscure losses when they occur. If their derring-do fails, the mistakes can be hidden in a variety of ways. A popular scheme is to create an entirely fictitious set of other trades that appear to neutralize the losses. When management asks why so much money is being paid out on the real derivatives positions, the traders say that it will be made up when the (fictitious) portfolio is sold.

A billion or so dollars later, word reaches management either from contrite traders or from suspicious auditors that the firm is financially ruined. At this point, the traders are fired. And that's it. Managers console one another about how they were collectively deceived, how it really wasn't anyone's "fault," and how they had all learned an important life lesson.

CONSTRUCTING A GOOD PLAN

In the foregoing scenario, a variety of fatal mistakes were made. Some of them are listed on the following page:

1. Management failed to become educated about derivatives; it simply bowed to financial fashion or perceived competitive threats.

2. No one in the hiring chain could intelligently assess the qualifications of the applicant trader.

3. The head trader was allowed to hire his or her "own people" with loyalty only to him or her.

4. The trading desk was allowed to isolate itself from the mainstream organization.

5. The trading desk was left largely unsupervised.

6. The traders were able to control the flow of information needed to monitor their activities.

7. Explanations given by the traders for large outflows of company funds were uncritically accepted; the supposedly countervailing "positions" were never verified.

8. No one in management felt responsible for the derivatives trading operation; everyone had a small role to play, but ultimate accountability was lacking.

9. Firing the traders was viewed as the "cure"; the obvious failure of the company to supervise that activity is not even acknowledged.

It is worthwhile to review each of these errors in their order of occurrence for clues (or "rules") on a better way to organize and to supervise a derivatives trading program. There is no single way, nor any "best" way. Systems must be tailored to the nature, structure, and personality of each organization. But regardless of the variables, the central objective is to *get control* over the trading program.

Rule 1: Get Up to Speed

This earliest step does not require that the company become an expert on derivatives. But someone within the organization should be assigned the responsibility to learn (or buy) knowledge sufficient to lead it into the derivatives area. In many cases, an outside consultant with extensive experience in derivatives will do nicely for this purpose, provided that the advice is objective (e.g., no headhunters, please).

This phase must predate any discussions with potential traders about employment. And it should examine *whether* as well as how to enter the derivatives business. The fact that competitors or rivals have entered the derivatives world does not mean that it is the best thing to do for your organization (or for theirs). And check out any stories of large profits or savings; there are braggarts everywhere.

Whoever performs this "expert" role should be seen as a *permanent* resource, not just an ongoing derivatives activity, and in training others within the firm for that purpose. As noted below, the head trader should *never* have ultimate control.

Rule 2: The Selection Process

Hiring anybody for any position is fraught with danger, of course. Choosing a derivatives trader is no exception. Indeed, because that person will likely handle large sums of money and have the ability to magnify its impact through leveraging of derivatives positions, special care is called for. It is important, therefore, to look for the following skills:

1. Knowledge of the markets
2. Trading acumen
3. Discipline, not only by behaving appropriately and ethically under market pressures but by complying with management policies

Knowledge of the markets broadly means an understanding of how the various derivatives instruments behave, what they can be used for, and where the buyers and sellers can be found. Trading acumen is the ability to react to profit opportunities in the derivatives markets and to cut losses at the appropriate time. This is an "art," of course, and only liars are 100 percent successful at it. But it requires a skill beyond an academic knowledge of the business. Finally, the discipline needed to operate a derivatives business successfully means having grace under fire in the markets and respecting company policies even when they hurt. The position of "cowboy" has no place in your company.

Derivatives traders are a nomadic lot. Because the pay can be very generous, traders may change jobs frequently. High job turnover, therefore, is not necessarily a warning sign for derivatives traders. At the same time, however, frequent job changes can signify that the individual is not a good trader, or that obeying company policies cannot be relied on, or that the personality of Genghis Khan is present. A thorough *background check* is imperative (checking with the current employer may not be enough—the employer may be delighted at the prospect of being rid of that person). There is also a good chance that the trader has been licensed at some time with the SEC, the CFTC, the NASD, or the NFA; any disciplinary history can be easily obtained.

The fact that a prospective derivatives trader appears to have an aggressive personality may not be a negative feature in that rough-and-tumble world. But it will almost surely mean that serious supervision will be needed, backed up by the organization's power structure. Don't expect some low-level worker or junior attorney to rein in the trader; any heart-to-heart discussions should involve an official with the acknowledged authority to hire and fire.

Rule 3: Everyone Is a Company Player

Because derivatives trading is so arcane, there is a natural tendency within organizations to view it as "different" from what everyone else is doing; GIs in World War Two probably felt the same about the Manhattan (atomic bomb) Project at Los Alamos. This is a dangerous attitude, made all the more so because the traders may actually *like* the resulting isolation. Taken out of the focus of most company programs, the derivatives trading desk may feel sufficiently liberated to engage in especially risky activity.

One key way to encourage this outcome is to give the head trader carte blanche to hire other derivatives personnel. More than the desk's budget needs to be controlled by management; vetting of new derivatives employees should require their exposure to a number of officials unrelated to the trading operation. The new personnel must be made to understand that they have been hired by the *company*, not by the head trader, and that they may therefore be fired, transferred, or otherwise dispatched at the company's will.

Even then, of course, a bond will develop between the head trader and the support staff. This is not only inevitable; it is also desirable. But care must be taken to assure that the derivatives operation does not become isolated from the rest of corporate life. There should be as much interaction as possible with other operating units, both professionally and socially. There should be a fairly natural kinship, for example, with the overall treasury function of the company, and there may be occasions when the derivatives desk needs help from the accounting area, marketing, etc.

Rule 4: Information Is Power

The saying "Information is power" has become a cliche in today's techie world, but it is a cardinal rule for the successful supervision of a derivatives trading operation. Nick Leeson kept Baring's Bank in the dark (bankrupting a 300-year-old bank), as did Mr. Hamanaka at Sumitomo ($2 *billion* in copper trading losses). Whatever information is needed by management to monitor the derivatives trading desk must be accurately and reliably available to it.

This means, at a minimum, the ability of management to verify *independently* what is happening on the trading desk. For exchange-listed derivatives, where transactions flow through a third-party broker, verification can easily occur by having management receive directly from the broker regular statements of trading activity on the derivatives desk. Since the accuracy of these statements is mandated by federal law, a high level of confidence can be placed in them. For O-T-C derivatives, however, tracking can be substantially more difficult. Since only the immediate parties prepare records of those trades, fabrication is a real risk. While management might seek to verify each trade by contacting the counterparty for confirmation, this approach is awkward (inferring a distrust of one's own personnel) and cannot detect whether a conspiracy is involved. Periodic audits are perhaps as effective a response as possible but are far from foolproof or fail-safe.

Care must also be taken to verify, whenever possible, all of the activity that the derivatives desk claims is taking place. If, for instance, the desk reports that a losing derivatives transaction was simply a "hedge" or "leg" for a broader trade including other instruments that eventually will generate comparable profits, it must be possible to confirm the existence of those other instruments. In one case, for example, a rogue trader explained huge losses in government bond futures by claiming to also own the bonds themselves; the company either did not or could not verify that statement even though it received a clear picture of the *derivatives* activity from various brokers. The bonds did not exist.

Rule 5: The Guillotine Effect

In the worst-case scenario described earlier, management basically held a wake after the losses had been incurred to console each other. The traders were fired, to be sure, but the effect was largely ceremonial; none of them could reimburse the company. And while the organization had filed away a marvelous manual of policies and procedures, absolutely *no one* could be held ultimately responsible for the catastrophe because their roles and duties as per the manual were too diffused.

In the supervision of derivatives activity, as in so many other arenas, accountability must have names next to it. Should a major snafu occur, specific people in the organization should bear the consequences, and, equally important, they should know it from the beginning. Monitoring will not work most effectively if blame-naming is left to the political survival skills of people after the fact.

And those within the company whose careers are at risk must not be confined to low- or middle-tier employees. Except in the most egregious circumstances, the chairman and the chief executive officer should probably be spared, but the next level need not be. A senior company officer who has been put in ultimate charge of the derivatives trading activity should have so much at stake that the program will work effectively; it always helps, of course, when that officer can dismiss anyone below. In that environment, supervision can generally be relied on to infect *every* subordinate level within the organization. This will throw the greatest light as well as the greatest heat on the derivatives trading desk, which, after all, is the objective.

To get the proper level of attention within the ranks, suppose the company submits for signature by senior managers the following resignation letter:

[Day/Month/Year]

Chairman and Members of the Board of Directors
ABC Corporation
1000 Risky Way
Termination City, Gone

Dear Sirs and Madams:

By this letter I hereby offer irrevocably to resign from all positions held at ABC Corporation, and agree to forfeit all benefits and entitlements associated therewith whether or not accrued or vested, at such time and on such conditions as you may determine in your sole discretion due to any violation by me or by any person subordinate to me of the policies of ABC Corporation governing the management (including supervision or oversight) or operation of ABC Corporation's derivatives trading or hedging program.

Sincerely,

[Name]
[Title/Position]

Has this lesson been learned? Consider Union Bank of Switzerland, which, in 1997, suffered derivatives losses of $418 million and was subsequently merged with Swiss Bank Corporation. The Swiss Federal Banking Commission investigated the episode but failed to censure *any* of the bank's officials; it was evidently deemed a sufficient response that unnamed employees who purportedly engaged in this "misconduct" were no longer with the bank. Although in this case there may have been extenuating circumstances leading to this outcome, a management that feels safe from the consequences of its derivatives traders cannot be expected to oversee that activity with the tenacity required.

CHAPTER 8

What the Pros Recommend

Chapter 7 took a practical, commonsense look at controlling the risks of participating in the derivatives markets. It should come as no surprise, however, that this subject has received close attention as well from the market watchdogs that have responsibility for the the safety of the international financial community—banks, brokerages, and corporations.

Particularly active in the area of risk management for derivatives have been the Basle Committee on Banking Supervision, an international group of government banking supervisors from major financial centers (e.g., the G-10 central banks), and the International Organization of Securities Commissions (IOSCO), which is a loose confederation of national securities regulators. Acting together, the Basle Committee and IOSCO have designed a framework which identifies the types of information that are important to monitoring derivatives risk exposure. Regulators in a number of major jurisdictions apply that framework in their own supervisory programs.

The recommendations of the Basle Committee and IOSCO address two levels of detail: (1) what data a manager should gather for continuous risk management purposes and (2) a subset of data to which regulators should have ready access. The former is characterized as a "catalogue" of data, while the regulators' focus is called (in predictable bureaucratese) "a common minimum framework of data elements."

The fundamental message of the Basle Committee/IOSCO study is simple enough: Information about derivatives activity should be *accurate* as well as *comprehensive* and *timely*. The study notes that collection of these data, however, may be complicated by the fact that derivatives activity is spread across different affiliates or is conducted in different countries or can only be fully assessed if other company operations (e.g., its regular commercial activities) are included in the risk "mix." The study further notes that the risk profile of derivatives positions can change swiftly and abruptly, requiring close monitoring at all times. This may be due to changing market conditions (e.g., interest rate fluctuations) or to the new, ever more exotic derivatives which the company is adding and for which a risk history has not yet developed. Furthermore, even in the case of a stabilized portfolio of derivatives, the exposure could increase suddenly because a countervailing transaction—for instance, a purchase of supplies whose cost was hedged by the derivative instrument—has concluded without disposing of the related derivatives.

The Basle Committee/IOSCO study suggests that data should be gathered and maintained on a current basis on the *magnitude* of the company's exposure to four major risks:

- Credit risk, or the possibility of counterparty default
- Liquidity risk, or the chances that an unwanted position cannot be closed out promptly or at a fair price
- Market risk, or how volatile the value of the derivatives may be (or become)
- Effect on earnings, or the impact of derivatives losses on the profitability and balance sheet of the company

CREDIT RISK

As noted elsewhere in this book, credit risk varies profoundly depending on whether the derivatives involved are exchange-traded or over the counter, because exchange-listed derivatives have an array of financial safeguards that largely make the participants indifferent to this risk—routine margining, daily marking-to-market of positions, and a clearinghouse last-resort financial guarantee. The Basle Committee/IOSCO study readily acknowledges this fact and recommends that more intensive monitoring of O-T-C derivatives is warranted.

It notes further that credit risk is not static; exposure to counterparty default may be remote in stable markets but can escalate dramatically with market volatility even when no change in the portfolio occurs. Thus, market developments can be a far better signal of derivatives credit risk than simply noting the face ("notional") value of the company's derivatives portfolio. And this risk cannot be viewed in isolation from other assets, investments, or activities of the company that may have elevated credit exposure under similar market or economic conditions. For the past several years, those assets may even include credit *derivatives* that the company has written or purchased. It is the *overall* credit risk exposure that is important.

Measuring *current* credit exposure requires a calculation of the *cost of replacing* the cash flows of profitable derivatives positions. Because it is now permissible in the United States and some other major jurisdictions to aggregate all derivative transactions with a defaulting counterparty, so that amounts owed *to* the defaulter can be reduced by the amount owing *from* that party, it is the *net* replacement cost that counts for this purpose. It is wise, whenever possible, to assure that each transaction is made subject to a netting agreement that can mitigate the size of a credit loss.

Calculating *potential* credit exposure is more complex than simply measuring current replacement cost for profitable derivatives. Exposure is affected by (1) price volatility estimates and (2) the remaining life span of the derivative instrument. Banks that operate under the 1988 Basle Capital Accord already apply a formula for this purpose (a so-called "add-on"), and similar measurements can be used by other derivative users. Or as some banks and securities firms have done, risk simulation models may be employed internally to test credit exposures; and while they can be quite sophisticated, they suffer—like all models—from the danger that the parameters used are not always correct or sufficient to the task.

Obviously, a little self-help never hurts, and it is quite common for derivatives parties to demand collateral as protection against default. In the exchange-traded world, the process is highly structured and vigorously enforced. For O-T-C transactions, however, greater flexibility exists, and the parties are largely free to negotiate a collateral arrangement which may call for immediate tender of the deposit, or for a deposit to be made if exposure grows beyond a defined limit, or for no deposit at all if counterparty credit risk is adjudged to be inconsequential. However, even where collateral is used, several concerns may arise. First, do I *really* (legally) have the right to keep the collateral if a default occurs; great care must be taken to assure that the security interest is enforceable against other claimants as a matter of law. Second, could the collateral lose value or even become worthless? In Russia, where government bonds were routinely used as margin for exchange-traded currency derivatives, markets were closed and trades were settled on an emergency basis when the government abruptly withdrew those bonds and announced an upcoming substitution of new debt in their place. Finally, how marketable is the collateral? The ability to liquidate the collateral quickly may be vital, especially if other obligations must be met from the proceeds.

Credit risk becomes more acute when it is concentrated in one or a few counterparties. At a minimum, careful records should be kept that will identify any such concentrations, and the level of current or potential exposure must be calculated frequently. Other dangerous concentrations might involve a particular sector of the economy (e.g., Japanese banks were made vulnerable by heavy lending in the real estate sector), or particular nations or regions of the world that might catch the same economic "flu" or suffer the same political turmoil, or (as in Russia) too much reliance on particular types of collateral. And, of course, high concentrations of credit risk in a single species of derivatives (e.g., interest rate swaps) threaten greater stress from the same economic event than a more diversified portfolio combining rate, currency, commodity, and/or equity exposures. The old reporter's admonition to always ask who, what, when, where, and how fits well in derivatives risk management, too.

The Basle Committee/IOSCO study also recommends that attention be paid regularly to the credit *quality* of counterparties, which can change quickly. Counterparties that have high levels of derivatives exposure, or that do not use netting agreements routinely, or that fail to demand collateral in circumstances where it would be prudent to do so, can suffer rapid credit deterioration. The quality of *their* counterparties is also important; defaults inflicted on them can set off a chain reaction as they become unable to meet their obligations as well. If possible, it is also wise to collect information from various sources about any slow-pay or past-due practices of a counterparty (or its counterparties), to monitor actual credit losses being sustained by counterparties, and to be sensitive to credit ratings assigned to counterparties by the major rating agencies like Moody's and Standard & Poor's.

LIQUIDITY RISK

"Liquidity" generally means the ability to eliminate an exposure quickly and at fair cost. The Basle Committee/IOSCO report further refines this concept to include exit impediments caused either by *market conditions* or by *scarcity of funds*. It reminds us again that greater market liquidity is likely to be found with exchange-traded derivatives (though not all are equally liquid) than with more "one-off" O-T-C instruments. Quick offset or liquidation can be impeded by (1) the uniqueness of the derivative, (2) the scarcity of suitable counterparties, or (3) the size of the derivatives position relative to overall volume in that product. The "notional" value of a derivative position is a poor indication of market liquidity; it may be relatively low as compared with overall market notional value but, due to lack of *trading volume,* may nevertheless be very difficult to liquidate.

Funding risk arises from the need to maintain sufficient cash flow to service all outstanding financial obligations. A counterparty default can severely interrupt expected cash inflow that was intended to service the company's own derivatives obligations. When the company seeks to maintain equal and opposite derivatives positions (called a "matched book"), the seeming neutrality of that strategy could be rudely disrupted if cash flows on either side were to be suspended. The Basle Committee/IOSCO study identifies certain practices that *may* be warning signs of funding problems: (1) unusual increases in the volume of options written (to generate immediate premium income though incurring additional market risk) or (2) the presence of swaps structured to generate a net cash flow at inception (again, quick cash for new risk). Moreover, the funding demands for exchange-traded derivatives are very evident and can be calculated because margin requirements are known and daily mark-to-market against price changes is easily measured. While more discretion exists with O-T-C derivatives and funding needs may therefore be less transparent, effort should be made to track changes in market conditions that may create cash flow stresses. For example, if O-T-C derivatives are hedged with exchange-traded products, funding demands could arise from the hedging operation even though the O-T-C positions seem fine.

Sudden changes in funding needs can be caused by factors other than market movements, of course. The Basle Committee/IOSCO paper notes that *contractual provisions* known as "triggering agreements" may exist between parties that require liquidation of derivatives or the posting of more collateral under certain circumstances, such as a credit rating downgrade. Accordingly, it is necessary to be alert not merely to the size of a counterparty's derivatives commitments but to their *terms* as well.

MARKET RISK

While this is clearly the most obvious risk taken by derivatives users, it is also one of the most difficult to measure. Markets rise and fall; when and in what way are imponderables that no one has mastered. While the Basle Committee/IOSCO report suggests disaggregating derivatives exposures even as finely as by individual portfolios, a single instrument, or the same maturity, it recommends that the objective of market risk measurement should be to assess the companywide exposures, including related cash market operations (e.g., activities being hedged with derivatives). It also recommends that regulators take advantage of the market risk models or systems employed by derivatives users to track their own exposures, although independent analysis is required as well to avoid compounding problems caused by imperfect internal modeling.

These assessments often include a breakdown of *types* of market exposures, to wit: interest rates, equity prices, foreign exchange (currencies), commodities, and options. In the banking community, for example, these categories are used to calculate the bank's minimum capital charge. The Basle Committee/IOSCO report indicates that a company's internal "value-at-risk" (VAR) methodology is useful in assessing market exposures and that, when derivatives users employ other approaches such as "earnings-at-risk" models, duration analysis, or stress scenario analyses, those data should be consulted as well.

VAR models seek to assess potential losses due to adverse market movements of a specific probability over a defined period of time and are widely used within the derivatives community and, in particular, by derivatives dealers and banks. The Basle Committee/IOSCO study recommends that VAR be measured over a period of time and that useful data could include identifying the highest VAR number during that period, or identifying monthly or quarterly averages of VAR over the period, but especially reviewing a time series of daily VAR estimates. And the efficacy of the VAR model should be tested periodically by comparing past VAR estimates with *actual results* in the derivatives portfolio. Using time series of VAR estimates, actual daily trading profits and losses, or other "back-testing" methodologies will validate or display faults in the VAR model; a significant disparity will warrant review of the model's assumptions or parameters.

It is also common practice for derivatives users to estimate the effects on their portfolios of low-probability adverse events (worst-case scenarios), known as "stress testing." For example, the portfolio might be assessed for impact if it had existed during earlier crises such as the 1987 stock market decline, the 1997 Asian financial crisis, or a period of extraordinary yield-curve abnormality.

It is important to note, however, that the "perfect" risk model has not yet been created. While some of the models are quite sophisticated and are being improved continually, there remains a need to use caution and common sense as well. It is difficult, for instance, to imagine an organization that has more expertise in derivatives than Salomon Smith Barney, and yet its parent, Travelers Corp., has curtailed certain of its trading operations because top management is uncomfortable with the risks involved, or is it with the difficulty of measuring those risks?

EARNINGS RISK

This is, clearly, the "bottom-line" concern. The *profitability* of derivatives activity is the final litmus test of whether the venture has been worth the bother. And yet "profitability" does not necessarily mean net gains from the derivatives themselves; where these instruments are used to hedge other activities, the combined result must be calculated. And revenue may result not only from favorable market movements; it may result from the initial calculation of market value ("origination revenue") or from changes during the period in the unearned credit spread.

Of particular concern in measuring earnings risk is whether losses are realized immediately or are deferred by the institution. Deferred losses may accumulate to imprudent size, can reduce expected future earnings, could erode the firm's capital position, and may suggest deficiencies in the company's internal controls. It is important to assess what valuation reserves and provisions for credit losses have been made that could cushion earnings losses without endangering the company's financial condition.

The Basle Committee/IOSCO study sets forth in Annexes 1 through 6 a series of analytical steps and explanatory detail that it views as "best practice" for assessing derivatives risk. Those annexes have been reproduced in Appendix C of this book.

CHAPTER 9

Preparing for the Future

To complicate further the life of an executive or manager who must stand vigil over the company's derivatives activity, consider how radically the *structure* of the derivatives community is changing today. It is not merely the derivatives instruments or "products" that mutate almost daily, but where, when, and how transactions are carried out will also be different tomorrow. As a result, no supervisory plan for derivatives risk management that is tailored to today's needs will fit snugly into the world of the future. This chapter identifies some of the structural changes that are under way within the derivatives community that will require users to adjust and to adapt their monitoring programs on an ongoing basis.

Developing an effective system of controls for derivatives activity is in part a function of how, at any given time, the business is structured. At present, the derivatives world consists largely of two "camps": the exchange-traded products and the over-the-counter instruments. Already a blurring has begun between O-T-C trading (done largely through proprietary computer terminals) and exchange-traded activity conducted on markets that use electronic execution facilities. To a trader, these environments are not materially different. Conversely, both are vividly different from open outcry trading on a number of the traditional organized exchanges. Those markets require a multistep process to effect execution, which may slow down the speed of trading and may add significant cost to the operation.

From a *supervisory* standpoint, however, the slower and more costly processes of open outcry trading may provide more opportunities to detect and to intercept errant activity before harm can occur. When each trading order must pass through several hands along the route to execution, and where the intermediaries assume financial responsibility in the process, more "eyes" follow each trade than will occur in an electronic environment where a trade may be "hit" instantaneously from the largely private and isolated location of a trader's own desk, and where predesigned warnings (like limits on trade size) may or may not be equal to the ingenuity of an aggressive trader.

THE RUMORED DEMISE OF OPEN OUTCRY TRADING

The conventional wisdom is that open outcry markets will soon be displaced by computerized screen dealing systems. Even today, most of the organized exchanges operate through the latter medium. In many cases, they came into existence as the technology was maturing and were found to be more attractive and more feasible than assembling the mass of human resources required to operate an auction system of trading. In some countries, like New Zealand, screen dealing was considered imperative because the market had two remote centers in Auckland and in Christchurch. And many of the European derivatives exchanges emerged in the 1980s under the sponsorship or encouragement of the local securities and banking communities that were already quite comfortable operating in an electronic environment.

Computer assistance is quite common in the O-T-C derivatives world as well. As a result, it seems likely that activity in the O-T-C and electronic exchange environments will gravitate toward each other. Indeed, because screen-based trading has no geographical center, it is possible that distinctions between "markets" in different cities will gradually disappear. If, for example, trading in Japanese equities (think Tokyo), in the futures contract on the NIKKEI stock index of Japanese equities (think Singapore), and in yen-denominated corporate debt (think London) can be accomplished by a single person from a single computer terminal, the geographical references become meaningless and there may no longer be any reason to use them.

Ultimately, there may be only a single "market" composed of a software package or Internet service allowing access to every available derivative product as well as to the underlying assets. Like current cable TV, there could be scores or hundreds of instruments on offer via the screen. It could become "the market," or, possibly, traders will stop thinking in "market" terms entirely. This trend should have only moderate impact on the O-T-C dealing community which is not market-centered even now, but the process of adaptation for traders accustomed to open outcry could be more challenging. Recall that these traditional markets offer more than execution facilities; they conduct self-policing (as insisted by the regulators), they develop new investment products, they conduct educational services, and, perhaps most important, they provide a financial guarantee through their clearinghouses.

DECONSTRUCTING THE TRADITIONAL EXCHANGE

With conversion to electronic trading and the decentralization of trading activity, it is possible to envision an "exchange" that is little more than a room housing a central processing unit with a handful of technicians on duty to fix any malfunctions that occur. How can any of the ancillary services of a traditional market be preserved under those circumstances? Electronic trading is an information and communication service that, like the telephone or e-mail, does not naturally offer any of these other benefits. New-product development will probably default to others who will be paid on a research-and-development basis. Education may pass to the academics. Self-regulation may be concentrated in a single organization having that dedicated purpose independent of the trading facility itself. But perhaps the greatest challenge will be replicating the guarantee function of a clearinghouse. After all, it is this feature that allows free participation by the broadest range of people; absent a financial guarantor the markets would be confined (as the O-T-C markets are today) to high-credit, top-tier reputation users only.

Historically, clearinghouses resembled associations of wealthy exchange member firms that pooled assets as financial backing for transactions on an exchange. In an electronic environment, there may or may not be such firms because their primary business—to act as intermediary between investors and the trading floor—could be largely displaced. In fact, a conversion to a screen-based trading system will provoke discussion about whether a member-owned structure is any longer either necessary or wise. In its place may arise a regular for-profit business corporation that is stockholder-owned and listed on a securities exchange, like many other enterprises engaged primarily in the telecommunications business. As a result, the very source of funds to provide a financial guarantee could be placed in doubt.

At the same time, the process of clearing entails not only a financial "safety net" to meet defaults but also a series of credit and payment controls designed to reduce to a minimum any risk of such defaults. This system has been summarized in Chapter 4 under "Timing Risk" and involves requiring an initial deposit of margin (good-faith funds), even before any losses occur; an adjustment of each account every day to reflect price changes and the collection of any losses; and a chain of financial responsibility beginning with the investor but passing serially through the hands of each carrying broker and clearing firm so that their collective capital stands behind the transactions before the clearinghouse itself is required to come to the rescue.

It is a reasonable assumption that no financial guarantee will be provided in the absence of those controls. Accordingly, if the traditional markets disappear, it may be necessary to replicate the functions of a clearinghouse in other ways. This will probably entail an extension of standby credit by a financial institution or consortium (the British banks once ran a clearinghouse that served a dozen or more exchanges around the world). The credit facility is likely to run in favor of selected organizations that have committed to impose credit and payment controls on their customers. These will be the same entities that will be required by regulators to intermediate transactions made by investors on the screen-based system (nearly every major financial regulatory agency has signaled that a licensed and approved intermediary will be required even for electronic trading). There is no perceived reason why a similar credit facility might not be offered to the O-T-C dealers as well, in which case public participation in that arena could expand enormously.

I was asked not long ago to narrate a possible reorganization of a traditional exchange after conversion to electronic trading. And so, while my prognostications have no greater credence than those of any other fortune-teller, I developed one process of restructuring that is designed to (1) maximize the liquidation benefits to former "members," (2) generate the greatest income (and lowest risk) for new investors in the business corporation, (3) replicate the self-regulatory and educational service through other means, and (4) develop an alternative clearing system, as follows:

Step 1: Privatizing Exchange Ownership

When operating a "market" required a pooling of human and economic capital at a central location, it made sense for ownership and control to rest with active trading or broking members. But an electronic trading system allows traders to disperse and to operate from almost anywhere. As a result, ownership of the exchange would be changed from a not-for-profit membership organization to a general business corporation with transferable shares held originally by the former members in the same proportions as their memberships bore to the overall number of exchange memberships. The shares' transferability would assure that former members could readily liquidate their holdings if they wish, or might increase their ownership interest through additional purchases of shares. This new entity could then serve as the "holding company" for most of the activities discussed below. In addition, the holding company could retain and exploit certain of the former exchange's assets such as its brand name or other intellectual property.

While the new shares might carry with them the right to trade on the electronic system, that outcome is not foreordained and holds certain disadvantages. Negative consequences of creating "trading shares" include (1) limiting the market for the shares to persons who can also qualify for trading privileges (i.e., a market among passive investors would be stifled); (2) creating a disincentive against issuing trading licenses to nonshareholders despite the substantial exchange revenues (and potential additional market liquidity) that could result; and (3) causing shareholder votes to be driven at least as much by the impact on their trading profits as by the exchange's own "bottom line." Another configuration would be to separate ownership from market access by reserving trading rights for licensing to qualified applicants; in that event, the shareholders would be entitled simply to the exchange's net distributed income from its various activities (transaction and clearing fees, licensing charges, ticker sales, research reports, etc.).

Of course, the economics of these new shares could be quite different from how memberships have traditionally been priced. The major factor in valuation of memberships historically has been in their perceived access to *trading profits* or *brokerage income,* not from the ability of the exchange itself to generate (and to distribute) operating income. Thus, equity would be separated from trading opportunities, with the latter reflected mainly in the price of trading licenses.

Step 2: Institutionalizing the Screen Dealing Mechanism

One subsidiary of the holding company would own (preferably) or license (second choice) and operate the screen dealing system. As in the past, its revenues would derive principally from transaction-related fees and sale of market data. This subsidiary might be wholly owned by the holding company or might share ownership with a third party, such as the system developer. In either case the allocate share of net income to which the holding company is entitled would be remitted to it by the subsidiary for possible distribution to the holding company's shareholders.

Step 3: Operating the Self-Regulatory Program

Assuming that the screen dealing activity will be subject to federal regulation, it would be necessary to organize a self-regulatory program including any screening of license applicants. That role might be performed by the subsidiary operating the computerized trading system, but a more flexible approach would be to create another affiliated entity for this purpose (similar to the NASDR unit of the National Association of Securities Dealers, Inc.), or even to contract self-regulatory services from a third-party provider (such as the National Futures Association). If a subsidiary or service provider is arranged for this purpose, it might also perform educational and training programs for the screen dealing market.

Step 4: The Clearing System

A separate subsidiary of the holding company could be created to act as clearer of trades made on the electronic trading system. As a separate entity, the clearer's exposure could be insulated legally from other affiliates. And insofar as trade processing and financial guarantees are valuable services, the clearer affiliate could generate considerable revenues ("clearing fees") as well. In addition, interest could be earned by the clearer subsidiary on idle margin deposits, as at present.

Thus far, the U.S. Commodity Futures Trading Commission has insisted that every designated contract market *must* employ a clearing mechanism. That regulatory requirement assures an ongoing need for the subsidiary's clearing services. Were the CFTC ever to relax that requirement (e.g., for institutional market participants), the clearer subsidiary could nevertheless offer stand-alone financial enhancement separately as a "product" to be purchased (or not) by traders, and might offer similar services outside the market as well (comparable to banks' sales of letters of credit). In other words, the clearer affiliate could serve as a general-purpose financial institution.

Note, however, that the clearer subsidiary would not likely operate under a system of mutualized risk; that is, it would not be funded through a pooling of capital by "clearing members" in the traditional sense. Presumably, it would operate through internal capital and reserves as well as lines of credit or liability insurance. Seed capital might be contributed by the holding company from the disposition of excess assets, as discussed below. And the clearinghouse's ability to liquidate undermargined positions on a marked-to-market basis should limit its exposure to manageable levels that outside funding sources would find acceptable.

Step 5: Liquidating Physical Assets

Conversion from open outcry to screen dealing would almost certainly eliminate the need for large quarters by either the exchange or its members. Thus, a very visible casualty of computerized trading is likely to be the facilities bought or leased to support open outcry floor operations. For markets that own real estate, a separate "liquidation company" owned exclusively by the former members could be formed to dispose of unneeded assets, and those sales should generate substantial cash for distribution to those members (a "liquidating dividend"). Alternatively, an agreed part of the distribution proceeds might be provided to the holding company to fund a clearinghouse or other continuing projects, with all remaining amounts to be distributed irrevocably to the former members.

The liquidation process might also include substantial revenues from the personal property that the exchange would no longer need. While one outcome would be to sell those assets piecemeal, a worthwhile search might be conducted for other potential users of the infrastructure "as is." Since the ultimate purpose of that infrastructure is to *process information* and to *conclude and record transactions*, there may exist other commercial organizations (e.g., a freight handler like FedEx or DHL, a joint airline reservation system, or a "just-in-time" supplier) that could adopt or adapt the existing facilities to their own needs. If so, the exchange would recapture not only a greater part of its investment in the personal property but some of the "intellectual capital" that had brought it together as a working system.

Step 6: Forming the Trading Firm

As noted earlier, the exchanges have assembled both trading capital and talent in concentrations that are hard to replicate. To preserve that value, the holding company could form a subsidiary for the purpose of trading the markets available on the screen dealing system (similar to a Goldman Sachs or Morgan Stanley), or an unaffiliated company could be created for that purpose. In either event, substantially all of the capital of the firm would be contributed separately by its trading partners and the profits would likewise be shared among them (maybe the holding company would absorb initial formation expenses or other costs from any liquidating dividend that it receives or in exchange for a minor profit participation).

Step 7: The R&D Subsidiary

As a traditional source of new-product development, the exchange has talented economists and marketers who might continue to conduct research-and-development work through a subsidiary of the holding company on a compensated basis. The output of these efforts would include both new-contract design and other market analyses that could be of use to the trading subsidiary or to outside customers.

As outlined above, the restructured "exchange" would consist of a holding company that was originally owned by all former members whose new shares are freely transferable, and that would exploit opportunities to license the exchange's name, trademarks, or other intellectual property as well as oversee the operations of subsidiaries separately engaged in the following:

- Systems operation and support
- Self-regulation and licensing
- Clearing and settlement
- Research and development

In addition, a company would be formed to liquidate the exchange's surplus property and assets, with the objective of a one-time cash distribution to the former members (with, possibly, a fraction to the holding company for funding its surviving services) by way of a "liquidating dividend." And, finally, a new trading house would be created for former members wishing to continue to capitalize a trading operation. If fully implemented, the resulting business structure could be depicted as follows:

Exchange Conversion
From Floor Trading to Screen Dealing

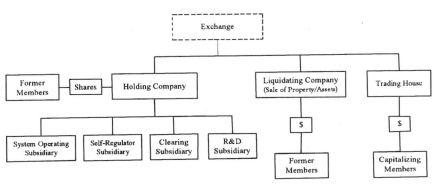

Whether it is appropriate to perform each of the operations discussed above through a series of *separate* subsidiaries would become evident over time, and some consolidation could occur where necessary. But because it is unclear at the initiation of the restructuring which of the market's "decomposed" services will be commercially viable in the long term, this approach is suggested so that any unsuccessful venture can be more easily jettisoned and any peculiar risks or legal exposures associated with one enterprise will not threaten the survival of other components. Of course, perhaps none of this will be needed after all, but just in case.

And upon due reflection, it seems obvious from this reincarnated creature that the distinction between "on-exchange" and "off-exchange" derivatives activity could largely evaporate.

PREPARING FOR REGULATORY CHAOS

Perhaps the greatest challenge in a futuristic world as is described here will be to the regulatory agencies. When the trading activity has no geographical locus, what national regulator is in charge? In the "old days," when the markets had fixed sites, the question was easily answered. With electronic systems, the identification of a lead regulator would become almost arbitrary. Should it be in the country where:

- The central processing unit is located?
- The relevant trading terminal exists?
- The relevant customer resides?
- The basis of a complaint arose?
- The executing firm is headquartered?

All of the above, and none of them, could be viewed as appropriate outcomes. As a result, regulators must begin to shed nationalistic orientations if possible in favor of a more global and unified system of supervision, and, in the end, a single regulator applying a single program to all electronic trading activity should emerge. Pollyanna? Perhaps, since it would become necessary to set aside patriotism, reject xenophobia, and attract cross-border funding. But if Europe has been able to unify key functions despite a long history of both oratorical and military belligerence, the creation of a global markets "cop" should be attainable.

Absent the classical member-owned and -operated exchange, the infrastructure to conduct a self-regulatory program—investigators, disciplinary committees, even the ability to impose penalties—may not exist either. An independent and dedicated self-regulatory organization would probably suffice if it enjoys sufficient resources. How will it be funded? If it operates for profit, shares might be sold to investors. If not, it might need to affiliate with the entities operating the trading systems which recognize the necessity of supporting a self-regulatory program in order to maintain the blessing of regulators.

Whatever twists and turns occur in the structure of the derivatives world, however, it is clear that there will be periods during which the changes themselves will generate uncertainty and confusion. The combination of electronic speed and regulatory inertia is explosive. The management of every organization in the derivatives markets during those times will be placed under special challenge to use self-help measures so that risks, both those normally encountered and the special risks of change, can be controlled effectively. A wise procedure is to review supervisory procedures on a regular basis and to ask in particular whether assumptions about the protections historically offered by regulators are still valid. If not, adjustments will need to be made to compensate for the shortfall.

CHAPTER 10

The Political Dimension

The derivatives business involves *big money,* which attracts politicians. As noted in Chapter 3, the organized futures and options exchanges have been subject to pervasive federal regulation beginning in 1922. By contrast, the over-the-counter derivatives dealers have largely avoided Washington's heavy hand since they first became a major factor in the 1980s. Because the central markets and the private O-T-C community now compete for many of the same customers, and with very similar products, the organized exchanges are often heard to complain that they do not enjoy a "level [regulatory] playing field" with the O-T-C dealers, and many skirmishes on Capitol Hill have occurred for that reason. This chapter undertakes to identify the principal "players" at the governmental level and to capsulize their interests and attitudes as manifested today.

When the CFTC was created through legislation in 1974, the futures industry fought hard to assure that its power went well beyond being just another regulator to worry about. The exchanges, led by the Chicago Board of Trade (my client at the time), wanted the CFTC's jurisdiction to be *exclusive;* in other words, they wanted the CFTC as their *only* regulator. Why? Because futures trading was expanding beyond the traditional grains and other farm products into metals, construction materials, foreign currencies, energy distillates, and, soon, securities in the form of a futures contract on

Government National Mortgage Association (Ginnie Mae) mortgage pass-through certificates and later on U.S. Treasury securities as well. If every federal and state agency having an arguable interest in any of those underlying assets could step forward to regulate futures trading in them, chaos might follow and the costs of compliance would soar. The industry's success in persuading Congress to award exclusive regulatory jurisdiction to the new CFTC has paid huge dividends ever since, although it has left a large number of federal and state regulatory wanna-bes spoiling for a rematch.

THE AGENCY PLAYERS

While the CFTC is the final arbiter of regulatory policy for the organized markets, it is mandated by law to consult with—and sometimes to seek concurrence from—other federal agencies on specific subjects. For example, on matters of U.S.Treasury securities futures or options, the CFTC must consult with the U.S. Department of the Treasury, which oversees the sale and supervision of those bonds, notes, and bills. Similarly, the CFTC must consult with the U.S. Securities and Exchange Commission on derivatives activity involving private securities that are generally regulated by the SEC; and in the case of futures contracts on stock indexes (e.g., Standard & Poor's 500 futures), the SEC has veto power over approval by the CFTC to trade those instruments.

On the perimeter of the derivatives business is also the Board of Governors of the Federal Reserve Board, which is consulted on a variety of fiscal issues and has the power (delegated to the CFTC) to set minimum margin requirements for stock index futures as well. Other, more remote, players include the Office of the Comptroller of the Currency, which sets some policy regarding use of the derivatives markets by national banks; the U.S. Department of Labor, which does the same for certain pension (superannuation) plans; and the General Accounting Office, which conducts studies of the CFTC's performance and recommends potential legislative changes.

The least stable relationship over the years has been between the CFTC and the SEC. The central derivatives markets have undergone a dramatic reorientation from their roots as agricultural hedging devices to become mainly a tool of the investment (aka securities) community. A wide array of futures contracts exist to-day on interest rate instruments that are debt securities, and some of the more popular futures contracts involve stock indexes like the S&P and the Dow that replicate the equity securities markets. The SEC has advocated on and off for two decades or more that it, and not the CFTC, should regulate these securities-based deriva-tives. While repeated efforts by the SEC in Congress to transfer this jurisdiction to the SEC have failed, the movement stirs on a periodic basis and can become a serious effort especially follow-ing dramatic market developments such as the October 1987 stock market crash.

In recent times, however, tensions between the CFTC and its fellow federal colleagues has had less to do with jurisdictional power grabs than with a philosophical difference of opinion whether certain segments of the derivatives world, especially the O-T-C community, should be regulated *at all*. The CFTC, which claims some regulatory jurisdiction over the O-T-C derivatives dealers by virtue of Congress's decision in 1992 to allow it to grant exemptions for that activity (see Chapter 3 for details), has indi-cated that it might develop a real regulatory structure for that com-munity. The Treasury Department, the Federal Reserve, and the SEC have cried "foul," arguing that the CFTC lacks any authority over that activity and, in any event, would be wrong to meddle in the O-T-C dealers' affairs even if it had a right to. In late 1998 they even prevailed on the Congress to enact legislation temporarily for-bidding the CFTC from regulating the O-T-C dealers.

While it might seem desirable to remain beyond the clutches of the CFTC, the O-T-C market could pay a hefty price for that libera-tion. Recall that those who are regulated by the CFTC are spared the nuisance of having to comply with demands from other federal and state agencies; this "exclusive jurisdiction" precludes many poten-tial threats, including the risk that derivatives transactions might be considered to be "gambling" under local laws, which could result in criminal prosecution or, at a minimum, might allow the losing party to renege on its payment obligation. As a result, a successful escape from the CFTC might be a race directly into the arms of other aspiring regulators.

While the CFTC (and the SEC, for that matter) was formed to be a hands-on, round-the-clock regulator of the futures and options business, neither the Treasury Department nor the Federal Reserve engages routinely in so intensive a supervisory role. While they take a keen interest in the national and state banks that are now very active in the O-T-C derivatives business (principally in swap transactions), the primary focus is on *fiscal soundness* rather than customer protection and other traditional regulatory goals. Accordingly, the Treasury Department and the Federal Reserve devote most of their attention to assuring that a bank's derivatives activity does not impact its safety and soundness; setting copious behavioral standards is out of character for them. This is why the O-T-C community rallies behind those agencies when questions of jurisdiction arise; it is unlikely that either government body will become an aggressive regulator.

CONGRESS

While the branches and agencies of the federal government joust over this issue, a parallel contest takes place in Congress. The CFTC's primary oversight committees in Congress are the House Agriculture Committee and the Senate Agriculture, Nutrition and Forestry Committee. As might be suspected, this role by farm-oriented congressional committees is a throwback to the early days of the futures exchanges when trading in grains and other agricultural commodities was the dominant activity. Although roughly 85 percent of all futures trading in the U.S. today involves items associated with other industries (principally Wall Street), the two agriculture committees have fought tenaciously to keep their pivotal role with respect to those markets. In part this is because agricultural futures, although a diminished percentage of overall volume, continue to be an important segment of the market. Whether the campaign generosity of the organized exchanges and their members has anything to do with it, or helps to explain the desire of other congressional committees to become more involved, is a matter for conjecture.

A consequence of vesting primary oversight of the CFTC in the two agricultural committees of Congress is the difficulty in naming the subcommittee that will be most intimately involved. In the Senate, the subcommittee name gives no hint of a CFTC responsibility: Subcommittee on Research, Nutrition, and General

Legislation. But in the House of Representatives the subcommittee's name suggests strange bedfellows indeed: Subcommittee on Risk Management (intended to signify derivatives) and Specialty Crops.

When issues arise about the CFTC's jurisdiction over particular activity that is arguably within the authority of another branch or agency of the government, demands may be made by other congressional committees involved with those other institutions to participate actively in any legislative process on the subject. When it could be asserted that the SEC has some authority over the activity in question, both the House Commerce Committee and the Senate Banking, Housing, and Urban Affairs Committee may insist upon holding hearings and contributing to the legislative process. Or where banks or banking interests might be affected, such as in the swaps business where banks are dominant players, the same Senate committee as well as the House Banking and Financial Services Committee may surface as interested parties. There can follow a tussle to determine what committees will take the lead; a *concurrent* referral of legislation to two or more committees in the same chamber infers equality among them, while a *sequential* referral identifies the dominant committee and subordinates the rest.

Participation in the legislative process by multiple committees of Congress generally prolongs the gestation period and can create a crowd scene when their representatives huddle to sort out disagreements in the Committee of Conference. From the standpoint of a potentially affected constituent, moreover, this contest of wills can produce bizarre results. I am reminded of a quotation attributed to an early American jurist, Gideon J. Tucker:

> No man's life, liberty or property are safe while the Legislature is in session.

Frequently, competing interests try to undermine each other and, failing that, to strike a compromise that may make no sense at all. Members of Congress may shift allegiances during these debates due to a change of heart or worse. By the end of the legislative ordeal any observer will understand what Otto von Bismarck meant when he said:

> If you like laws and sausages, you should never watch either one being made.

THE STATES

As noted earlier, the grant of exclusive regulatory jurisdiction to the CFTC also neutered the various states that had ambitions to regulate the derivatives world. The State of California had already enacted a specific law governing trading in commodities, and many states had been invoking their local securities ("blue sky") laws in an effort to control that activity. The 1974 federal legislation put an end to state intrusion, with limited exceptions such as prosecution under general criminal laws. In subsequent years, Congress cautiously broadened the states' ability to attack wrongdoing in this field but did not permit the development of any formal regulatory programs. Repeatedly the states petitioned Congress to restore their ability to conduct local regulation, frequently arguing that they are best situated to "get the crooks" operating within their territories. Ironically, most of these advocates managed the states' securities commission or agency that often was not allowed to go to court; indeed, in some states like New York, only the Office of the Attorney General could do so. As a result, much of the states' aggressive talk was seen as mere bravado, and few inroads have been made into the CFTC's domain.

As discussed earlier, the *absence* of CFTC jurisdiction leaves room for states to invoke any and all of their laws, rules, and regulations. Members of the O-T-C community, which fought so hard in the early 1990s to be exempted from most CFTC requirements, must now concern themselves with whether other federal or state laws could apply to them. For example, in the case of a catastrophic loss derivative, where investors stand to lose money if a defined disaster occurs, issuers of these instruments are generally exempt from CFTC requirements but as a result must now worry about whether state *insurance* laws might be invoked against the transaction. Even so, it would be fair to ask whether any type of business would actually *seek* CFTC regulation for this reason. Oddly, the answer is "yes." In 1974 a small group of commodity firms using a sale technique similar to a "layaway" purchase plan for precious metals— known as leverage contract merchants—devoted months of effort to assuring that they were *included* within the CFTC's exclusive jurisdiction, hounded to that desperate strategy by zealous state securities regulators and consumer protection units that had brought many lawsuits against them. It remains to be seen whether, over time, the unregulated O-T-C derivatives business will be forced to do the same.

The politics of derivatives is complex. No exchange or O-T-C dealer can credibly threaten to amass votes against a member of Congress in the next primary or general election. The derivatives community has no grass-roots power and therefore cannot interact with Congress the way that, say, a large labor union can. Moreover, the derivatives world is quite difficult for ordinary people to understand; even the jargon is confusing. What little sentiment regarding derivatives that can be discerned among the general public is likely to be hostile anyway.

Under these circumstances, it should come as no surprise that the principal weapon of the derivatives business is—money. While generous campaign contributions leap to mind (fund-raising on Wall Street has always been a pleasant experience for politicians), there are other money cards to play as well. In a city like Chicago where the largest futures exchanges are situated, tens of thousands of jobs are dependent on that business; in New York City where most O-T-C dealers will be found, the same impact on the local economy could be felt. To a senator, a member of congress, a mayor, or a city council member, the specter of retarding derivatives activity through overzealous or imprudent legal strictures is unacceptable not only because of the risk of high unemployment but also because of the likely erosion in the tax base that supports so many unrelated government programs. On one occasion when the City of Chicago and the State of Illinois were contemplating imposing a tax on every exchange transaction, the Chicago Board of Trade considered moving to another location (for some reason, Dallas became the relocation focus). The taxes were not then, nor have they ever been, adopted.

Finally, the CFTC plays an important role of constituency stroking for members of the two congressional agriculture committees. Many of those members are from farm states where the agricultural community is suspicious of the organized derivatives markets. Voters observe on their TV screens the bedlam of activity by crowds of people in the Big City, many of whom have never seen a farm, setting prices without regard for the farmers' best interests. They also see (and many are appalled by) the specter of city slickers getting rich from a drought or a famine. The members receive criticism from time to time from back home for appearing to be too "cozy" with those exchanges. A judicious visit by CFTC officials to the member's district, an occasional appearance on local television, or a speech at the co-op goes far in allaying the constituents' anxieties; there *really is* a cop on the beat after all. Every chairman of the CFTC has been called upon to perform this function, a request that it would be imprudent to refuse.

THE MEDIA

Derivatives have never lived in harmony with the news media. First, they are easily misunderstood because of their complexity, so all manner of misconceptions can flourish and feed preposterous news stories. Second, there is a natural suspicion about people who make their living *pretending* to be someone else—a gold prospector, an oil wildcatter, a stock wizard, or a scion of high finance— when they do not really conduct those businesses. Nor does it help the industry's image that, during the most somber or cataclysmic moment, a TV news crew can tape the floor of a derivatives exchange where hundreds of screaming, flailing traders appear to be either celebrating or conducting a feeding frenzy in response to the tragedy.

The media intersect with politicians all the time, including those legislators and government officials who have the power to hurt the derivatives industry. From time to time, the media will focus on the derivatives community in an effort to rile up the public. Perhaps it takes the form of a blazing headline or TV "exposé" suggesting corrupt practices on the exchange floors. Or it may be a crusade to blame the derivatives markets for the level of producer prices (too low) or consumer costs (too high). The CFTC itself was created in 1974 in part because Congress thought that the Department of Agriculture (the predecessor regulator of these markets) had failed to prevent Chicago "speculators" from boosting soybean prices to over $12 a bushel. But the CFTC has not fared much better; its markets have been blamed for allowing silver prices to reach $60 an ounce in early 1980 and even for the October 1987 stock market plunge. It sometimes seems that derivatives have been associated by the media with just about every catastrophe known to humanity except global warming (and perhaps a link will be found there as well).

Derivatives are here to stay. It is difficult to imagine managing finances or conducting business without them these days. But they are not to be trifled with. Many are highly complex and behave in sometimes unpredictable ways. And new architectures are being developed continually. Yesterday's derivatives have advanced through many generations of innovation so that, today, a request that would once have produced the financial equivalent of a sling-shot will now beget a nuclear device.

Populating the derivatives world are a band of risk takers who, oddly enough, frequently trade to transfer risk to others. But most people are risk-averse, and this includes nearly the entire spectrum of management within companies that use derivatives. Their aim is to avoid becoming a casualty of that process. Despite best efforts, that aspiration may be defeated. The best defense against this *career risk* is effective supervision of the derivatives activity so that calamities do not occur.

This book has sought to provide some guidance toward that end. And if any further reinforcement is needed, read Appendix A, which follows, on the Baring's Bank debacle that was prepared by the Bank of England for the House of Commons. It should dispel any illusions that derivatives disasters cannot happen to nice people who *think* they are good managers.

Report of the Board of Banking Supervision [Bank of England] Inquiry into the Circumstances of the Collapse of Barings

RETURN TO AN ORDER OF THE

HONOURABLE THE HOUSE OF COMMONS DATED

18 JULY 1995 FOR THE

REPORT OF THE

BOARD OF BANKING SUPERVISION

INQUIRY INTO THE CIRCUMSTANCES

OF THE COLLAPSE OF BARINGS

Ordered by The House of Commons to be printed 18 July 1995

1. Introduction

Summary history, structure and principal activities of Barings

1.18   At the time of the collapse Baring Brothers & Co., Ltd (BB&Co) was the longest established merchant banking business in the City of London. Since the foundation of the business as a partnership in 1762 it had been privately controlled and had remained independent. BB&Co was founded in 1890 to carry on the business of the bank in succession to the original partnership. In November 1985 Barings plc acquired the share capital of BB&Co and became the parent company of the Barings Group. In 1991 the Barings Group acquired a 40% equity interest in Dillon, Read & Co Inc (Dillon Read), a US investment bank based in New York.

1.19   The voting share capital of Barings plc was held by its executive management and the non-voting share capital was held by the Baring Foundation, a UK registered charity.

1.20   In addition to BB&Co, the other two principal operating companies of Barings plc were Baring Asset Management Limited (BAM), which provided a wide range of fund and asset management services, and Baring Securities Limited (BSL), itself a subsidiary of BB&Co, which generally operated through subsidiaries as a broker dealer in the Asia Pacific region, Japan, Latin America, London and New York. Appendix VII includes charts setting out the corporate structure of the Barings Group as at 31 December 1994. BAM and the corporate finance activities of BB&Co are not referred to in any detail in the report as they are not considered relevant to the inquiry. Hereafter, when we refer to Barings we mean BIB and its component companies and operating units, principally BB&Co and BSL.

1.21   BB&Co was an authorised bank, based in London, with branches in Singapore and Hong Kong. BAM also owned two banks: Banque Baring Brothers (Suisse) S.A. and Baring Brothers (Guernsey) Limited.

1.22   The business of what became BSL was acquired from Henderson Crosthwaite by BB&Co in 1984. BSL was incorporated in the Cayman Islands, although its head office, management and accounting records were all based in London. BSL had a large number of overseas operating subsidiaries including two which are of particular relevance to this inquiry, namely BFS and Baring Securities (Japan) Limited (BSJ).

Regulatory environment

1.23   The Barings Group's operations across the world were subject to the supervision of a variety of different supervisors. Of these, only supervision by certain UK, Singaporean and Japanese supervisors are relevant to the inquiry.

1.24   The Bank authorised BB&Co (which was therefore an authorised institution) under the Act to accept deposits. The Bank was therefore responsible for monitoring whether BB&Co continued to meet the criteria set by the Act for its continuing authorisation. The minimum criteria for authorisation are contained in Schedule 3 to the Act and the most relevant are summarised in Appendix XIV. The Bank was also responsible for the consolidated supervision of the Barings Group. This entailed the receipt and analysis of data on the consolidated (Group-wide) capital ratios and consolidated large exposures and the assessment of the risks to BB&Co emanating from the non-bank parts of Barings; it did not entail actual supervision of the non-bank parts of the Group. The limits on the Bank's responsibilities in respect of its role as the consolidated supervisor of the Barings Group are described in more detail in Section 12.

1.25   The SFA, as a self-regulating organisation under the Financial Services Act 1986 (FSA), authorised BB&Co, BSL and Baring Securities (London) Limited (BSLL) (from its establishment in 1993) to carry out certain types of investment business in the UK. The SFA has a duty to regulate the investment businesses of its member firms conducted in the UK in order to afford an adequate level of protection for investors. Accordingly, the SFA regulates its members in relation to: their financial resources; the security of investors' money and assets held by members; and the fair and proper conduct of investment business undertaken. The regulation of the financial resources of BB&Co was delegated by the SFA to the Bank under a Memorandum of Understanding (MoU) in April 1991, a copy of which is attached as Appendix VIII.

1.26   BFS was a corporate clearing member of SIMEX. SIMEX is a self regulatory organisation for the financial futures industry in Singapore. The approval for the establishment of SIMEX as a futures exchange was granted by the Monetary Authority of Singapore (MAS) under the Singapore Futures Trading Act. SIMEX is primarily concerned that its members are financially sound and are professional in their dealings with other members.

1.27   BSJ was licensed by the Japanese Ministry of Finance (MoF). It was also subject to the rules and regulations of the self-regulatory exchanges on which it traded.

The auditors

1.28   The Barings Group financial statements were the subject of an annual external audit pursuant to the Companies Act 1985. The purpose of the annual audit is to report to the shareholders on whether the financial statements give a true and fair view of the state of affairs and results of the group concerned and comply with applicable UK company legislation. The auditors of Barings plc, BB&Co and BSL at the relevant times were C&L London.

1.29   For the financial periods ended 30 September 1992 and 31 December 1993 the auditors of BFS were the Singapore firm of Deloitte & Touche (D&T), who were succeeded for the financial year ended 31 December 1994 by C&L Singapore. At the time of the collapse C&L Singapore had substantially completed its audit of BFS for internal group reporting purposes and had reported to the directors of Barings plc, but had not reported on BFS's statutory financial statements.

1.30   For the financial periods ended 31 December 1992 and 31 December 1993 C&L London had audited and reported on the Barings Group financial statements. At the time of the collapse C&L London's audit of the consolidated financial statements of Barings plc and the financial statements of BSL for the year ended 31 December 1994 was well advanced, but they had not yet issued their formal report on those financial statements.

Barings' management

1.31 The management structure of Barings at the time of the collapse is described in Section 2. The Board of Directors of Barings plc (the Board), under the chairmanship of Mr Peter Baring, met six times in 1994. The Executive Committee of the Board (EXCO), also under the chairmanship of Peter Baring, met weekly to consider the key business issues and decisions affecting the Barings Group. The Management Committees of BIB (under the chairmanship of Mr Andrew Tuckey, Deputy Chairman of Barings plc and Chairman of BIB) and BAM were given a high degree of autonomy to make decisions relating to their business units. Mr Peter Norris was the Chief Executive Officer of BIB (CEO designate from December 1993, CEO from November 1994) and a Director of Barings plc (from December 1993), having previously been CEO of BSL.

1.32 In February 1994 the Board appointed an Audit Committee comprising three non-executive directors. Previously, the whole Board had an annual meeting with C&L London. By the time of the collapse the Audit Committee had met only once, in June 1994, to receive a presentation on the management letter by C&L London in respect of the year ended 31 December 1993 and a report from BB&Co's Internal Audit Department. No matters relating to BFS were discussed at that meeting.

Background to BFS's trading activities

1.33 BFS, a Singaporean registered company, was an indirect subsidiary of BSL. BFS was originally formed to allow Barings to trade on SIMEX. At the time of the collapse BFS employed 23 staff. BSL's other significant Singaporean subsidiary was Baring Securities (Singapore) Pte Limited (BSS) which employed some 115 staff. BSS's principal activity was securities trading.

1.34 BB&Co and BSL issued a number of comfort letters to the MAS and to commercial banks which lent funds or securities to BFS. The purpose of the letters was to assure the recipients that Barings would financially support BFS. For example, in a minute of a BSL board meeting on 16 April 1991 it is recorded that the directors resolved to issue such a letter to the MAS. Included within the proposed wording was the

statement: "[BSL] accepts full responsibility for the operations of [BFS]. . . In addition to our legal responsibility de-
riving from our shareholding in [BFS]. . . [BSL] will ensure
that [BFS] maintains a sound liquidity and financial position
at all times, and we will, on demand, provide adequate funds
to make up for any liquidity shortfall in [BFS]". The letter
of comfort later issued to the MAS was the same as the
proposed wording in all material respects.

1.35 From late 1992 to the time of the collapse BFS's General
Manager and Head Trader was Leeson. Prior to his move to
Singapore in March 1992, Leeson worked for Barings in London in a back office capacity for almost three years. A more
comprehensive description of his career and background is
included in paragraphs 2.55 to 2.60.

1.36 Barings sought to control and manage its operations by
means of a 'matrix management' system, a not unusual
method of management control for financial businesses
which have global operations. Managers who are based
overseas often have local reporting lines (typically of an administrative nature) as well as reporting lines to a product
manager (who may be based at the business' head office or a
regional office). Leeson reported to Barings' management in
Singapore for BFS's office infrastructure, in particular to Mr
James Bax, Regional Manager South Asia and Director of
BFS, and to Mr Simon Jones, Regional Operations Manager
South Asia, also Director of BFS and Chief Operating Officer
of BSS. Jones and the heads of the support functions in Singapore also had reporting lines to the Group-wide support
functions in London. Whilst there was some debate about
Leeson's precise reporting lines (paragraph 2.27), from 1 January 1994, for product profitability, Leeson reported to Mr
Ron Baker, Director of BB&Co and Head of the Financial
Products Group (FPG) of BIB, via Ms Mary Walz, one of Ron
Baker's London based managers and also Director of BB&Co
and Global Head of Equity Financial Products, BIB. Section 2
of the report sets out the conflicting views which existed as
to Leeson's precise reporting lines within Barings during his
time in Singapore.

1.37 From mid-1992 BFS executed trades on SIMEX (in Singapore) and OSE, TSE and TIFFE (all in Japan). BFS primarily executed trades in three kinds of financial futures contracts (namely: the Nikkei 225 contract, the 10 year Japanese Government Bond (JGB) contract and the three month Euroyen contract), and some options on those same financial futures contracts. The market prices of these contracts were related to the price or value of the underlying Japanese securities. For example, the price of the Nikkei 225 contract was related to the value of the Nikkei 225 index of leading Japanese companies' share prices. The products are described in Appendix V. Since SIMEX was created in 1984 it has developed parallel markets for these products in direct competition to the Japanese exchanges on which they are traded. Thus, the three products in which BFS primarily traded could be traded on one of the Japanese exchanges or on SIMEX or both, and the different characteristics and rules of the exchanges (described in Section 3 of the report) gave rise to advantages for certain customers to deal on one exchange in preference to the other.

1.38 BFS's original function was to execute trades on behalf of Barings' clients. Most of these clients were clients of either BSL or BSJ, and the trades were booked by BFS in the name of BSL or BSJ. This is commonly known as 'agency' business, and was managed by Mr Mike Killian, Head of Global Equity Futures and Options Sales, BIB, from Tokyo and latterly the United States. BFS would generate revenue from the commission it charged clients for this type of trading. Barings' records show that in mid-1993 BFS began to generate profits from trading for Barings' own account ('house' or 'proprietary' trading) by purporting to take advantage of price differences between SIMEX contracts and the equivalent contracts on the Japanese markets. This is commonly recognised as a form of arbitrage trading, and was called 'switching' business by Barings.

1.39 The reported profits from this trading were significant. We describe in Sections 4 and 5 how the reported profits from this activity from January 1993 to the collapse were in fact offset by much greater losses which were actually being incurred and which were concealed.

1.40 The trading conducted by BFS on these exchanges required very substantial funding in the form of margin payments to the exchanges to support the positions held by BFS. At the time of the collapse BFS's unaudited balance sheet recorded that it had placed some £468 million with SIMEX as margin. Most of this funding was provided by BB&Co via BSL and BSLL or by BSJ. This funding is described in Section 6 of the report.

1.41 Until the collapse, Barings' management in London believed the trading conducted by BFS to be essentially risk free and very profitable. They believed that BFS entered into equal and opposite matched positions on a particular contract on SIMEX and one of the Japanese exchanges, and reasoned therefore that the net value of the two holdings would not be affected by price movements on the exchanges. However, as is set out in Sections 4 and 5, BFS did not in fact hold matched positions and the value of its positions was substantially affected by price movements on the exchanges.

Events leading up to the collapse

1.42 In March 1992 Leeson was transferred from London to Barings' operations in Singapore. After passing local examinations, he himself began trading on the floor of SIMEX. At about the same time, or in early 1993, he was appointed General Manager of BFS.

1.43 In July 1992 account '88888' was opened in BFS's records as a 'client' account. As we describe in Sections 4 and 5, this account was used to conceal the unauthorised trading activities of BFS through 1993, 1994 and up to 23 February 1995.

1.44 In July and August 1994, a BSL internal audit team of three visited Singapore to perform a review of the operations of Barings' offices in Singapore and other nearby countries. BFS's operations were reviewed by one member of the team, Mr James Baker, an Internal Audit staff member, BSL. The report of the visit was finalised in October 1994. It identified, among other items, that there was a lack of segregation of duties between BFS's front and back offices. The report, and the issues arising from it, are described in Section 9.

1.45 By January 1995 management of Barings in London became aware of market concerns and rumours regarding the scale of

Barings' trading activities on OSE (Section 7) and the possibility that Barings had a customer who could not meet a margin call. Barings received a telephone call on 27 January 1995 from the Bank for International Settlements (BIS) who had heard rumours to the effect that Barings had margin losses in the Nikkei contract and could not meet its margin calls. These market concerns and rumours do not appear to have caused management undue alarm because management thought that, unbeknown to the rumour mongers, Barings' positions were matched with equal and opposite positions on SIMEX.

1.46   In January 1995 SIMEX noted from its financial surveillance programme that BFS appeared to be financing the positions of clients, in particular those in account '88888'. On 11 January 1995, SIMEX wrote to BFS, in Singapore, asking for an explanation for this.

1.47   From late January 1995 the size of the gross matched positions entered into by BFS on SIMEX and the Japanese exchanges increased, as reported to the Barings Asset and Liability Committee (ALCO) in London which discussed the associated funding issues and the market perception of Barings' positions. On 26 January 1995 ALCO instructed that Leeson be ordered not to increase and, where possible, to reduce the size of the positions, but these instructions were not complied with in the period up to the collapse.

1.48   On 27 January 1995 C&L Singapore faxed a note to C&L London which identified that there was an amount of ¥7.778 billion (some £50 million) in BFS's 31 December 1994 balance sheet apparently due from Spear, Leeds & Kellogg (SLK), a New York based specialist and securities trader. On or before 1 February 1995 C&L London informed Mr. Geoffrey Broadhurst, Group Finance Director, BIB, of this supposed transaction. This supposed receivable was identified by us as one of the techniques used by Leeson to conceal the balance on account '88888' which recorded the unauthorised trading activities. We describe it in more detail in Section 7, and deal with its use in concealment in Section 5, with its relevance to external audit in Section 10 and with its relevance to large exposure reporting to the Bank in Section 11.

1.49 On 31 January 1995 ALCO in London discussed a letter dated 27 January 1995 from SIMEX to BFS, a copy of which had been sent to London. The letter presented a summary of BFS's positions at 30 December 1994, and reminded BFS of its responsibilities to ensure that it had sufficient funds to enable it to fulfill its financial obligations to SIMEX.

1.50 On 3 February 1995 Bax sent a memorandum to Norris, Broadhurst, Ron Baker, Mr Ian Hopkins (Director and Head of Group Treasury and Risk, BIB (from 23 August 1994) and Director of BB&Co) and Mr Tony Gamby (Settlements Director, BIB (from 1 January 1994), and Director of BB&Co) headed "SIMEX" and reading in part: "As you know recent incidents have highlighted the current operational weaknesses of our SIMEX business and an urgent need for a new approach . . . The growing volumes traded on SIMEX have meant Leeson can no longer continue to run the trading and settlement roles effectively. In any case, it has long been acknowledged that there are control weaknesses in this arrangement". The incidents referred to were not explained in the memorandum but clearly included a reference to SLK.

1.51 In the week beginning 6 February 1995 Mr Tony Hawes, Group Treasurer, BIB, visited Singapore with Mr Tony Railton, Futures and Options Settlements Senior Clerk, BIB, in an attempt to resolve a number of issues. Tony Hawes told us his agenda was to:

(a) understand the issue raised by Barings' auditors, C&L, in relation to the large purported debtor of some ¥7.778 billion (£50 million), (referred to in paragraph 1.48), in BFS's 31 December 1994 balance sheet;

(b) finalise a written response to the letter dated 27 January 1995 from SIMEX to BFS, in which SIMEX had sought reassurance from Barings as to its ability to fund large payments to SIMEX at short notice;

(c) brief his colleague, Railton, on: "improving the bookkeeping and treasury in Singapore so that we would receive in London information that would allow us to identify what all the margin they were putting up there was for and to ensure that we were funding it correctly, we would know which clients we were lending money to and provide all the information which had been lacking up to that point"; and

(d) arrange larger daylight overdraft facilities with local banks.

1.52   Railton told us that he felt that he was sent out in order to understand how the BFS Settlements Department worked and to provide cover for Ms Norhaslinda Hassan, the BFS Senior Settlements Clerk, who was on maternity leave.

1.53   Tony Hawes spent the week of 6 February 1995 in Singapore. He was unable to resolve the first of his issues, but did not believe the matter was urgent as he was told that the apparent debtor (SLK) had since repaid the funds to BFS. He knew that he was coming back to Singapore two weeks later and was prepared to resolve it then, leaving a list of questions for Leeson to answer in the meanwhile. He finalised the reply to SIMEX and met their representatives. He left Railton with some work to complete in Singapore and returned to London.

1.54   Railton was asked by Tony Hawes to complete a spreadsheet the purpose of which was to analyse the timing of the different types of margin which had to be paid to SIMEX by BFS.

1.55   Over the course of the week beginning 13 February 1995 Railton realised: "If you close out all the positions there is absolutely no way on God's earth that you could actually return all the yen". He described to us his increasing concern at what he seemed to be discovering. He told us that towards the end of the week he informed Mrs Brenda Granger (Manager of the Futures and Options Settlements Department in London, BIB), Gamby and Tony Hawes of this problem. He recalled informing Granger and Gamby of his estimated shortfall, ¥14 billion (some US$140 million). At this stage no misfeasance seems to have been suspected.

1.56   It was also during the week of 13 February 1995 that Railton discovered that the breakdown of the US Dollar margin funding requests which BFS had been submitting to London was meaningless. He had, in fact, had concerns about these requests since late 1994. Railton told us that BFS knew the total US Dollars that they wanted and that Ms Nisa Kader, BFS

Settlements Clerk, Singapore: "was just changing the figures [in the breakdown analysis] to meet the total". On 17 February 1995, following this discovery, Railton introduced a new form of margin request. Railton told us that around this time it became clear that: "half the stuff I had been advised on as to how it [the spreadsheet] worked did not work. . . The project was becoming more and more complicated the further one went along. I advised Brenda [Granger] of this, and I said, 'I really am stuck now because we are missing this 14 billion [Yen]' ".

1.57 According to Granger, Railton reported to her on 17 February 1995 that his reconciliation, of what he thought ought to be on deposit with BFS's bank or as margin on SIMEX and what was actually there, did not reconcile, and that the funds at SIMEX and the bank were US$190 million less than the amount recorded in the BFS accounting records as owing to BSL, Banque Nationale de Paris (BNP) and BSJ. Railton recalls the figure as ¥14 billion, Granger ¥19 billion (US$190 million); we believe they are describing the same reconciliation problem and only differ in their precise recollection of the difference. Granger told us that Railton was now "really worried". Railton still believed at this stage that the difference may have been due to his lack of understanding of the relatively complex BFS margining system, although by this time he believed that only Leeson could answer his questions.

1.58 By the third week the reconciliation problem remained unresolved. Railton told us that he was relieved that Leeson (whom he had not been able to see before to discuss the position in any detail) had eventually agreed to see him on the Monday morning. However, Leeson was reported to be ill on Monday and Tuesday (20 and 21 February 1995) and did not appear at the BFS office.

1.59 During the evening of Wednesday 22 February 1995 Railton met Leeson at BFS's office and recalls telling him: "we were missing this amount of yen, and he said 'Yes, I agree with you', which took me back a bit". Leeson then identified more detailed information that would need to be produced, although the matter remained unresolved.

1.60   The next morning, Thursday 23 February 1995, Railton went to SIMEX to see Leeson. Leeson gave him some explanations, but due to the noise of the exchange and because Leeson carried on trading, Railton did not feel that it was worth carrying on the discussion and returned to BFS's office. That afternoon Leeson came back to the BFS office, sat down with Railton and Jones and started to discuss the situation. After 20 to 30 minutes Leeson left the office. Railton thinks this was at about 4pm to 4.30pm. Railton recalls continuing to discuss the matter with Jones and Miss Rachel Yong, Financial Controller, BSS. Railton recalls Jones saying: "I do not blame you for wanting to speak to Nick [Leeson]. This does not make any sense to me". In the event Leeson did not return to the office.

1.61   On the evening of Thursday 23 February 1995 Leeson and his wife are believed to have travelled to Kuala Lumpur from where he faxed, on Friday 24 February 1995, a letter to Bax and Jones in which, according to Bax, he wrote that: "he was sorry, his health was deteriorating and therefore he wished to resign". From there Leeson and his wife flew to Kota Kinabalu. On Wednesday 1 March 1995 they flew to Frankfurt, where Leeson was detained by the German authorities on Thursday 2 March 1995. Leeson has been charged with offences under the Criminal Procedure Code of Singapore and the Singaporean authorities are seeking his extradition from Germany.

1.62   In London, on Thursday 23 February 1995 Gamby, to whom Granger reported, was told by her that: "Nick [Leeson] was coming back to the office later on in the evening to ensure that the reconciliation was done". Around midday (London time) on that day Gamby recalls hearing that Leeson could not be tracked down. Later that afternoon Gamby told Norris that they had: "a US$170 million reconciliation problem, but, more to the point, we could not find the trader".

1.63   On Thursday 23 February 1995 Tony Hawes flew from Tokyo on his planned return visit to BFS, arriving in Singapore at 2am Friday (Thursday night in London). He told us that, on arrival at his hotel in Singapore: "The phone rang almost immediately. It was Peter Norris from London asking me 'what on earth was happening in Singapore and where was Leeson?'". Tony

Hawes met Railton, who had also been called by Norris, and went to the offices of BFS. They started trying to reconcile the cash position, and Tony Hawes concluded that the apparent settlement of the SLK year end receivable (paragraph 1.48): "had been manufactured". They were joined by Bax and Jones. Tony Hawes started looking at a computer printout and noticed an: "account called an error account with goodness knows how many transactions on it, all of them seemingly standing at enormous losses". This was the account '88888' which was used to conceal losses from Barings London. It is described in more detail in Sections 4 and 5.

1.64 Norris contacted Walz in an attempt to locate Leeson. Walz eventually spoke to Leeson's mother-in-law who told her that Leeson and his wife had called a couple of hours earlier to say that they were going to Bangkok for the weekend. As Gamby said: "That was really when the alarm bells started flashing". In London that Thursday evening a group including Broadhurst, Granger, Gamby, Mr. George Maclean (Head of the Bank Group, BIB, and Director of BB&Co), Norris and Walz continued discussing the reconciliation. Mr David Hughes, Treasury Department Manager, BIB, who worked for Tony Hawes, told us that on the Thursday evening: "I got called into Peter Norris' office. News was then breaking that there was a significant problem. . . As you can imagine, all kinds of speculation was occurring at that time". The team in London worked through the night: "looking at the positions". Early the next morning Norris instructed Gamby to travel to Singapore to verify the situation reported by Tony Hawes and, according to Gamby: "to see, hope against hope, if there was some client sitting behind the '88888' account that we were not aware of". Gamby travelled to Singapore with Granger and Mr Mike Finlay, who also worked in the Futures and Options Settlements Department in London. His team worked through Saturday night, and confirmed what Tony Hawes had uncovered, namely that BFS was apparently insolvent.

1.65 At some stage over that weekend the Barings team working in the office of BFS forced open a drawer in Leeson's desk. Railton told us: "There was a stack of paper. There were holes in some. You could see how he had produced [the] confirmation of the SLK deal, I believe, and also I think a bank statement as well". Granger told us she was there and: "He [Bax] opened the folder and there was this fraudulent document". Gamby also said that in Leeson's drawer: "We found some cut and paste material for the SLK transaction. There was this SLK letter with a scissor cut around the signature. . . we also found a cut and paste of a Citibank statement". The significance of these documents is described in Section 5.

1.66   Meantime, on the morning of Friday 24 February 1995 certain Barings plc directors met in London and, having taken legal advice, decided that the Barings Group could continue to trade through that day. At noon on Friday Peter Baring met the Bank's then Deputy Governor and informed him that he considered that Barings had been the victim of massive fraud. The Governor returned immediately from holiday and vigorous attempts were made to save Barings over the weekend, but, owing in part to the uncertain cost of closing the open positions when the markets reopened on Monday morning and the related difficulty in establishing the facts about Barings' financial state, these efforts were unsuccessful. As a result, three partners of Ernst & Young (E&Y) were appointed as administrators of Barings plc and certain of its subsidiaries in the late evening of Sunday 26 February 1995. In Singapore, on Monday 27 February 1995, partners of Price Waterhouse were appointed by the Singapore High Court (the Court) as Judicial Managers of BFS, when BFS failed to pay a margin call.

1.67   Just over a week later the majority of the assets and liabilities of the Barings Group were purchased by Internationale Nederlanden Groep N.V. (ING), the large Dutch banking and insurance group, although BFS remains under the control of the Judicial Managers.

Indicators

1.68   This report identifies a number of warning signs which were available to Barings' management concerning the nature of the activities undertaken by BFS. The most significant indicators are set out in paragraph 1.70. The indicators vary in their weight and an individual item taken on its own may not have raised alarm. Taken together, however, we consider that they provided

Barings in Singapore and London (some of them during 1993 and 1994, and all of them by January/February 1995) with significant warning signals of the danger to which it was exposed.

1.69 Careful analysis of these indicators is important. There were substantial realised and unrealised losses resulting from BFS's unauthorised activities in 1993 and 1994. The information provided to the inquiry indicates that, at 31 December 1994, the cumulative concealed losses were £208 million. The majority of the trading losses incurred by BFS's activities occurred in 1995 (Section 4); the loss at 27 February 1995 being £827 million. If management had identified and realised the significance of the unauthorised activities in Singapore, depending on the date of discovery, Barings might have been saved from insolvency (although it would still have incurred a very substantial loss).

1.70 The indicators as identified by the inquiry are:

(a) The identification of the lack of segregation of duties in BFS between front and back offices, which was subsequently reflected in the internal audit report following the review of BFS's operations which was conducted in July and August 1994;

(b) The high level of funding required to finance BFS's trading activities;

(c) The unreconciled balance of funds (the 'top up' account) transferred from Barings in London to BFS for margins;

(d) The apparent high profitability of BFS's trading activities relative to the low level of risk as perceived and authorised by Barings' management in London;

(e) The discovery of the purported transaction relating to an apparent receivable of ¥7.778 billion (approximately £50 million) from one customer (SLK) of BFS as at 31 December 1994;

(f) The letter sent by SIMEX to BFS on 11 January 1995 (which was not communicated to London at that time), which included specific reference to account '88888' and its large funding requirements; and the letter sent by SIMEX to BFS on 27 January 1995 (which was communicated to London) in which SIMEX sought assurance regarding BFS's ability to fund its margin calls should there be adverse market movements;

(g) Issues and questions arising out of Barings' reporting of large exposures and client money to supervisors and regulators;

(h) The high level of inter-exchange arbitrage (or 'switching') positions without any application of gross limits; and

(i) Market concerns circulating in January and February 1995.

Limitations on access to documents and individuals

1.71 The inquiry has not had unfettered access to all relevant directors and employees of the Barings Group and its records, or to third parties who hold, or may hold, relevant information. Indeed, we have not been able to perform some important investigation work. The position is summarised in the following paragraphs.

1.72 In London, we have been able to interview all relevant directors and employees of the Barings Group. Although we have not had direct access to the offices of the Barings Group, we have been provided with copies of all the significant documents that we requested, with the exception of certain electronic mail messages which apparently have not been retained. We had requested access to Barings' electronic mail messages (either stored in hard copy or electronic form) sent and received by certain members of management and staff at Barings in London and BFS. We are informed that not all of these messages were routinely stored. In the case of messages sent from BSL's offices in America Square in November 1994 and January 1995, the computer tape archive is either missing or is corrupted. We have not had any access to electronic messages archived by BFS. Accordingly, we have not had full access to this source of information. During our investigation, we also requested access to telephone records and recordings for certain members of staff and management of the Barings' offices in London, Singapore and Tokyo. Barings' policy, generally, was to record the telephone lines of dealers, settlements staff and selected other personnel. In the course of our work we reviewed the telephone recordings available for Walz, Mr Fernando Gueler (Head Proprietary Equity Derivatives Trader, BSJ) and Mr Adrian Brindle (FPG Trader, Tokyo) for the period 23 January 1995 to 27 February 1995. Additionally we obtained transcripts of calls made by Ron Baker in New York during the period from 26 January 1995 to 27 January 1995. We were not, however, granted access to any telephone recordings made in Singapore which might have included lines for Leeson, Bax and Jones. Individuals who had taped lines may have chosen to take calls on or transfer calls to other extensions which were not taped.

1.73 In Tokyo, we have had free access to all the relevant documents, directors and employees of BSJ. BNP, whose Tokyo office was the only external client of BFS, has not permitted the inquiry access to its employees or documents.

1.74 In Singapore, we have been provided with copies of a limited number of documents by BFS and SIMEX. There remain a number of very significant categories of documents which we have not been permitted to examine, including BFS's bank statements. Similarly, while we have spoken to some BFS directors and employees on a brief and informal basis, we have not been permitted by the Judicial Managers (see below) to interview any of these important witnesses, while they remain in Singapore, nor to review any tape recordings of BFS telephone calls. Almost all the figures, analysis and conclusions in Sections 4 and 5 are derived from the inquiry's analysis of a photocopy of the '88888' account statement originally found by Tony Hawes. We were also given a copy of the same document by Jones. To verify this information we would need access to further SIMEX statements, BFS's records and selected BFS directors and employees. Since the collapse, a number of individuals and entities based in Singapore have had control of access to relevant documentation and individuals. The current situation in relation to each is as follows:

(a) Judicial Managers—The Judicial Managers retain custody of the majority of BFS's records. They initially provided some documents, but thereafter did not permit the inquiry team access to any further documents requested, nor have they permitted interviews of BFS's employees without directions from the Court. An application for directions to be given access to information held by the Judicial Managers was therefore made on behalf of BoBS to the Court on 27 April 1995. The Court declined to give the directions requested principally because insufficient commercial benefit could be shown to accrue to BFS as a consequence of the proposed exchange of information between the inquiry and the Judicial Managers. The Judicial Managers did not support this application nor did they oppose it. However they did permit Bax and Jones to make representations to us in response to our notification of our provisional conclusions;

(b) Singapore Inspectors (the Inspectors)—The Inspectors, who are partners of Price Waterhouse, were appointed on 10 March 1995 by the Singapore Minister of Finance to investigate the collapse of Barings under their Companies Act. The Inspectors have not given the inquiry team access to the documents and information they control because they maintain that there is no 'gateway' for them to disclose information to any party other than their Minister of Finance. The Singapore Minister of Finance, in turn, has not permitted the inquiry access due, we understand, to legal constraints in Singapore. The joint administrators of Barings plc have given the Inspectors access to documents and members of staff in London. As a person appointed under Section 41 of the Act, Mr Watt has been able to obtain copies of transcripts of those interviews the Inspectors conducted in London. The investigation team has met the Inspectors and their representatives to discuss particular aspects of the investigation. While they did not provide the inquiry with any documents, apart from the transcripts, this has gone some way to assist the inquiry in overcoming the difficulties caused by the lack of access to documents and individuals in Singapore. However, there remain significant areas in which we lack information;

(c) Commercial Affairs Department (CAD)—CAD is responsible for conducting the criminal inquiry into BFS's and Leeson's activities in Singapore. They have a number of relevant documents under their control. CAD did not permit the inquiry access to these documents without approval from the Judicial Managers of BFS, which was not forthcoming;

(d) C&L Singapore—We have not been permitted access to C&L Singapore's workpapers relating to the 1994 audit of BFS or had the opportunity to interview their personnel. C&L Singapore has declined our request for access, stating that its obligations to respect its client's confidentiality prevent it assisting us;

(e) D&T—We have not been permitted access to the D&T workpapers relating to the 1992 and 1993 audits of BFS or had the opportunity to interview their personnel;

(f) SIMEX and Citibank (Singapore)—We have approached both institutions in an attempt to verify the authenticity, accuracy and completeness of the transactions recorded in the '88888' account statement we have obtained. SIMEX would be able to provide an independent record of BFS's dealing, and Citibank copies of BFS's banking records. Initially SIMEX provided some statements of daily transactions by BFS, but, apart from that, both institutions informed us that the Judicial Managers, to whom obligations of confidentiality are owed, would not consent to the release of further information to the inquiry; and

(g) SIMEX—We have not been permitted to see the detailed supervisory working papers relating to SIMEX's supervision of BFS, nor to interview SIMEX's staff responsible for that supervision (paragraph 12.161).

1.75 In Appendix" IX we describe the steps we have taken in attempting to gain access to the information held in Singapore.

1.76 The inquiry has identified a number of third parties with whom BFS and Leeson in particular had a trading relationship. The investigation team has had limited discussions with some of these parties, but has not been able to examine their detailed trading records freely or conduct interviews with them.

1.77 Leeson has been invited to cooperate with the inquiry, but has declined to do so as long as he remains liable to be extradited to Singapore. There are no available means of compelling him to assist. Through his solicitors, he has been informed of the conclusions we have reached about his part in the collapse. His solicitors in a letter dated 22 June 1995 have replied to us: "We note the preliminary conclusions reached by your enquiry relating to Mr Leeson. These conclusions are inaccurate in various respects. Indeed, in relation to certain of the matters they betray a fundamental misunderstanding of the actual events. Unfortunately, given the uncertainty regarding Mr Leeson's position we are not able to provide you with a detailed response to your letter". Since receipt of this letter we understand that information has been provided by Leeson through his solicitors to the Serious Fraud Office (SFO) pursuant to undertakings of confidentiality which does not enable the SFO to pass this information to us. We have received no communication from Leeson since his solicitor's letter of 22 June 1995 that his unwillingness to respond to our requests for information or our invitations to comment upon our conclusions has altered.

Implications of limited access

1.78 The implications of not having had access to the information described above are as follows:

    (a) we have not been able to verify with Leeson the strategy which lay behind the unauthorised trading conducted by BFS or to understand his motivation;

    (b) we have not been able to verify the entries (and therefore the losses) on account '88888' against records held by SIMEX;

    (c) we have not been able to exclude the possibility—that anyone else at Barings (Singapore, London, Tokyo or elsewhere) was involved in this unauthorised trading;

    (d) we have not been able to exclude the possibility that third parties were involved in unlawful activities with any employees of Barings;

    (e) we have not been able to exclude the possibility that any of the funds sent by BSL, BSLL and BSJ to BFS have been misappropriated;

    (f) we have not been able thoroughly to investigate the management roles of Bax and Jones;

    (g) we have not been able to review and conclude on the adequacy of the work performed by BFS's auditors; and

    (h) we have not been able to review and conclude on the adequacy of SIMEX's supervision of BFS's activities.

1.79 The contents of this report are based on information to which we have been able to obtain access, including that provided to us in interviews. In view of the limitations on access to information which we have described, it is possible that material new facts may subsequently come to light. Despite these limitations, we consider that we have been able to ascertain the causes of the collapse of Barings, and to identify some important lessons for the future. . . .

14. Lessons arising from the collapse

LESSONS FOR MANAGEMENT

Management teams have the duty to understand fully the businesses they manage

14.8 Senior management is responsible for directing the business which, for many financial institutions, has become increasingly complex and diverse. What is essentially the same business may now operate in a number of financial centres and marketplaces, through varying legal entities and under different legal and regulatory' jurisdictions. Also, the reliance on trading activities to generate an increasing proportion of total revenues has changed the nature of risk for many institutions within the industry. Rapid product innovation and sophisticated technology, alongside vastly improved communication systems, have to be understood and managed actively.

14.9 At Barings, neither the top management nor the relevant members of the management of the FPG had a satisfactory understanding of the business that was purported to be transacted in BFS, despite the significant profits that were reported and the funding that it required.

14.10 Barings' experience shows it to be absolutely essential that top management understand the broad nature of all the material activities of the institution for which they are responsible and that product management have a detailed understanding of all aspects of the activities they manage. This detailed understanding must include a thorough and continuing analysis of the risk and potential return of each product, how they relate to one another, and the type of control systems required to reduce the risk of error or fraud to a level acceptable to the institution. Management must demonstrate in their everyday actions their belief in, and insistence on, the operation of strong and relevant controls throughout the institution. This is particularly important in high volume, volatile products where the associated risks are correspondingly higher. This understanding, which is no less important in the case of an area of business which is perceived to be very profitable, can be gained through an appreciation of the specific market characteristics, the risks the institution faces, the competitive position of the institution in the relevant marketplace, the identity and requirements of customers, and the basis of the reported profits and risks.

14.11   It is important for the relevant managers to make visits with reasonable frequency to overseas offices engaged in trading, especially where the office is geographically remote from the head office. These visits should include discussions with traders, risk managers, office managers and support staff about the activities, and talking to competitors and other institutions in the market (such as exchanges), about the perceptions of the institution's activities and traders. It is only with an understanding and feel for the business that management will be able to ensure that it receives the right information and can ask the right questions. Senior managers at Barings did not have this level of understanding and also did not enquire into the activities of BFS in sufficient depth, even when a number of warning signals arose.

Responsibility for each business activity has to be clearly established and communicated

14.12   We have described in Section 2 of our report the ambiguities that existed in Barings concerning the reporting lines of Leeson. Whatever form of organisational structure is chosen by an institution, clearly defined lines of responsibility and accountability covering all activities must be established and all managers and employees informed of the reporting structure. The identification of accountability extends beyond profit performance to encompass risks, clients, support operations and personnel issues.

14.13 All institutions should maintain an up-to-date organisational chart which shows clearly all reporting lines and who is accountable to whom and for what. There must be no gaps and no room for any confusion so that the situation of one manager believing another manager has responsibility for an issue, and vice versa, is avoided. Each individual in the institution should have a job description which clearly identifies his or her responsibilities and to whom and for what he or she is accountable. It is often said that the de facto reporting lines are determined by those who propose or set remuneration levels. It is therefore important that this is recognised when forming the organisational structure, especially when a substantial portion of an individual's income is in the form of bonus.

14.14 The need for clarity in accountability becomes increasingly important in a structure where an individual is responsible to one manager for a certain part of the business and to one or more other managers for other aspects of the business. This form of organisational structure is commonly referred to as a 'matrix' and was used by Barings. We make no criticism of the matrix style of management and, indeed, would observe that many institutions successfully operate such a matrix.

14.15 Nonetheless, there are some specific lessons to be learnt from the Barings collapse for organisations which operate a form of matrix structure. First, in a structure which has responsibility for products on a global basis and responsibility for operations on a local basis, the integrity of the controls over the activities of the local office must not be compromised. This means that the management of the local office must have a clear understanding of the business that is being conducted within the sphere of their geographical responsibility, notwithstanding reporting lines which are established along product lines. While local management may not be involved in day-to-day business decisions, it should have the authority to act to ensure that standards of control prescribed by the organisation are adhered to. Secondly, activities which are out of the mainstream may not find a natural home in the organisational structure and the risks of such activities being unmanaged and unsupervised is thus increased substantially.

Close attention must therefore be given to ensuring a proper level of management control is exerted over such activities. Thirdly, because of the distribution of accountabilities and responsibilities in a matrix style organisation which involves dual reporting lines, effective communication between senior managers is essential.

14.16   When an institution is making significant changes to its organisational structure, as in the case of Barings during the two years prior to the collapse, the risk of there being a lack of accountability for parts of the business or ambiguities in reporting responsibilities is substantially increased, particularly when the reorganisation involves bringing together business units having very different characteristics and management cultures. It is therefore important when an institution is moving from one structure to another, that senior management ensure lines of responsibility are clear and that there is independent monitoring of internal controls at each stage of transition.

Clear segregation of duties is fundamental to any effective control system

14.17   Perhaps the clearest lesson that emerges from the Barings collapse is that institutions must recognise the dangers of not segregating responsibility for 'front office' and 'back office' functions. Clear segregation of duties is a fundamental principle of internal control in all businesses and has long been recognised as the first line of protection against the risk of fraudulent or unauthorised activities. In the exceptional case of segregation of duties not being feasible due, for example, to the small size of the operation, controls must be established such that they compensate for the increased risks this brings, including close and regular scrutiny by internal audit. Management should also be wary of situations where it is apparent that only one individual is able to field all the key questions about a particular activity.

14.18   The term 'back office' typically covers trade entry, settlements and reconciliations. By necessity, it is often the case that 'back office' personnel work closely with traders on a day by day basis. However, this close and necessary working relationship must not develop to the point where the 'back office' becomes subordinate to the traders, as it appears happened in BFS. Institutions should have documented procedures and controls covering all aspects of transaction processing, accounting and reporting. Personnel who are asked to deviate from these should question why, and if they are dissatisfied with the answer given should be encouraged to report the matter immediately to senior management.

Relevant internal controls, including independent risk management, have to be established for all business activities

14.19   A breakdown in, or absence of, internal controls at a basic and fundamental level enabled Leeson to conduct unauthorised activities without detection. Each institution must determine for itself the controls most relevant and applicable to its business. However, we draw attention to aspects of control which the collapse of Barings confirm are of crucial importance.

14.20   A significant lesson concerns the failure of Barings London adequately to establish and verify the purpose of various large payments to BFS before they were processed. A basic principle of prudent management is the maintenance of robust systems of verification and reconciliation in the settlements function, irrespective of whether the payments are to group companies or third parties.

14.21   A particular concern in the case of Barings was that the funding from London to Singapore, much of which purported to be on behalf of clients and which therefore apparently generated client credit exposure, was not subject to the same rigour of checks and verification as if the payments had been drawdowns on a standard loan arrangement. All institutions should ensure that they have controls to identify the points at which a credit exposure may arise and to ensure that the exposure has been properly approved before payment is made. The sum of individual client loans should be reconciled to the total client loans shown in the balance sheet on a regular basis. Institutions which have acquired or developed securities businesses should take particular care to ensure that they have adequate controls over credit risk, an area which was weak in Barings.

14.22 A related matter concerns the co-mingling of house and client monies in payments made for margin. Institutions should distinguish between payments made on behalf of the house and those on behalf of clients: whenever possible before payment, but, failing that, as soon thereafter as possible, so that the necessary checks can be performed and the correct accounting entries raised.

14.23 A number of industry studies have strongly advocated the establishment within a financial institution of an independent risk management function overseeing all activities, including trading activities, and covering all aspects of risk. We support this view.

14.24 A primary objective of the risk management function is to ensure that limits are set for each business. These limits should reflect the risks being run and the level of risk that management is willing to take. The function also should serve as an independent check to ensure that traders operate within their limits; that exceptions are reported and actioned promptly; that sensitivity to changes in the market and their impact on the value of the position are assessed and reported; and should ensure that profits and losses are regularly recomputed and reconciled to the accounting records and, if necessary, the records maintained by the traders.

14.25 Unlike the situation at Barings, where Group Treasury and Risk focused on market and credit risk, an independent risk management function should oversee all types of risk. These other risks include: liquidity risk, concentration risk, operational risk, legal or documentation risk and reputational risk. Senior management in particular should be concerned about the risk of its institution attracting an adverse reputation and the impact of that on its business.

14.26 For the 'switching' activity, Barings only considered outright market risk (i.e. net long or short positions), reflected in the close of day market risk limit of zero and a small intra-day market risk limit. They did not establish gross position limits for each side of the 'switching' positions. Furthermore, an arbitrage business such as 'switching' attracts basis risk between two different markets (i.e. price movements are not one hundred percent positively correlated)

and also exposes the institution to the settlement characteristics of these different markets, creating liquidity and funding risk. The events at Barings show the need for institutions
to consider setting gross limits in respect of their arbitrage
activities. Institutions should also consider allocating funding limits amongst its activities, relating them to the various
risk limits.

14.27   Barings erroneously concluded that BFS's activities were
low risk. Higher risk activities not only necessitate stronger
and more extensive internal controls but also provide opportunities for higher remuneration levels for employees
engaged in, or managing, them. We do not consider it is for
us to suggest to institutions how they should reward their
management and employees and, if there is a bonus element
in the remuneration arrangements, how the bonus should
be calculated, shared and paid. However, we would note
that the opportunity to earn significant bonus based on revenue or profit, in relation to base salary, emphasises the need
for vigilance in the design of the systems of internal controls.

**Top management and the Audit Committee have to ensure
that significant weaknesses, identified to them by internal
audit or otherwise, are resolved quickly**

14.28   A few months prior to the collapse, Barings established a
group internal audit function. Prior to that the internal audit
functions in the bank and in the securities business were separate and there was no effective communication between
them.

14.29   For institutions engaged in a variety of activities we consider
that the internal audit function should be established or over-
seen at group level. This would facilitate critical issues or
weaknesses being communicated to top management on a
timely basis and enable the head of internal audit to plan or
review the allocation of resources across the entire group. The
greater the size, risk, complexity or geographical spread of
the business, the greater the need for experienced internal auditors with strong technical abilities and expertise in the relevant market sectors.

14.30   Internal audit should coordinate its activities with the external auditors and communicate key findings to them. The head of internal audit should have unrestricted access to the Chief Executive Officer, Chairman and the Chairman of the Audit Committee, irrespective of the person to whom he or she reports. Internal audit should be a core part of an institution's control systems and we think it essential that it is accorded a status in the organisation which it often lacks. One of the responsibilities of the Audit Committee should be to satisfy itself on the effectiveness of the internal audit function.

14.31   By the time of the collapse, neither senior management nor internal audit had followed up to ensure the implementation of the management actions as agreed following the recommendations in the October 1994 internal audit report on BFS. In preparing internal audit reports, major control weaknesses should be highlighted, and a management action plan to remedy the weaknesses should be agreed with a timetable. It is the responsibility of management to implement internal audit recommendations and, when major issues arise, to ensure they are remedied expeditiously. In the case of significant weaknesses, internal audit should plan return visits within a short period of the completion of the audit to ensure corrective action has been taken. Failure of management to implement recommendations within a timeframe agreed with internal audit should be reported to the Audit Committee.

Excerpts from the *United States General Accounting Office Report on Derivatives Losses Where Sales Abuses Were Alleged*

OTC Derivatives Losses Involving Sales Practice–Related Lawsuits

No.	Entity or individual reporting losses	Loss amount (millions)[a]	Specific type of derivative product	Relevant lawsuit claims, defenses, or counterclaims	Dealer	Outcome of lawsuit
1	RCS Editori (Italy)	$371	Interest rate and currency swaps	Fraud, breach of fiduciary duty, and fraud under Italian securities law	Bankers Trust	The parties settled for an undisclosed amount.
2	Henryk de Kwiatowski	$300	Currency forwards and options	Breach of fiduciary duty; negligence; fraud; negligent misrepresentation, breach of contract; and various violations of the CEA, including fraud in connection with the sale of commodities for future delivery (section 4b), fraud by a commodities trading advisor (section 4o), and dealing in illegal off-exchange futures	Bear Stearns	Ongoing. In a ruling on the defendant's motion to dismiss, the U.S. District Court for the Southern District of New York allowed to stand the plaintiff's claims related to breach of fiduciary duty, negligence, and the count relating to fraud by a commodities trading advisor (section 4o). The court's ruling dismissed the claims of fraud, negligent misrepresentation, breach of contract, and the other CEA-related claims of fraud under section 4b and illegal futures dealing.

No.	Entity or individual reporting losses	Loss amount (millions)[a]	Specific type of derivative product	Relevant lawsuit claims, defenses, or counterclaims	Dealer	Outcome of lawsuit
3	State of West Virginia	$280	Treasury options	Fraud	Greenwich Capital Markets, Goldman Sachs, Morgan Stanley NatWest Government Securities, and Salomon Brothers	The other dealers settled with the state for a total of $28 million, but after a jury trial in the Circuit Court of Appeals of West Virginia overturned the lower court's ruling and ordered a new trial. Morgan Stanley subsequently settled with the state for $20 million.
4	Procter & Gamble	$157	Interest rate swaps	Fraud, breach of fiduciary duty, negligence, misrepresentation, fraud in connection with the sale of a security under the Exchange Act, and violations of the CEA's general fraud section (4b) and fraud by a commodities trading advisor (4o)	Bankers Trust	In ruling on a motion by Bankers Trust, the U.S. District Court of the Southern District of Ohio dismissed or found in favor of the dealer on all securities and commodities law counts and left counts related to fraud and contract validity to be tried. On the day the ruling was issued, the two parties settled, with Bankers Trust forgiving about $150 million of the $200 million that it was owed by Procter & Gamble.

No.	Entity or individual reporting losses	Loss amount (millions)[a]	Specific type of derivative product	Relevant lawsuit claims, defenses, or counterclaims	Dealer	Outcome of lawsuit
5	PT Dharmala Sakti Sejahtera (Indonesia)	$64	Interest rate swaps	Misrepresentation, breach of contract, breach of duty of care, and transaction conducted with unauthorized end-user personnel	Bankers Trust	The Commercial Court of England ruled in favor of Bankers Trust, indicating that the dealer owed no duties beyond that of ensuring that the facts in any representations were made fairly and accurately. The parties subsequently settled for an undisclosed amount.
6	Minmetals	$52	Currency options and swaps	Fraud, breach of fiduciary duty, transaction conducted with unauthorized end-user personnel, and fraud under the Exchange Act and the CEA	Lehman Brothers	Ongoing.
7	UNIPEC	$44	Currency swaps	Fraud, breach of fiduciary duty, transaction conducted with unauthorizedend-user personnel, and fraud under the Exchange Act and the CEA	Lehman Brothers	The parties settled for an undisclosed amount.
8	Seita	$30	Interest rate and currency swaps	Misrepresentation, breach of fiduciary duty, negligence, and breach of contract	Salomon Brothers	Ongoing.

No.	Entity or individual reporting losses	Loss amount (millions)[a]	Specific type of derivative product	Relevant lawsuit claims, defenses, or counterclaims	Dealer	Outcome of lawsuit
9	Laszlo Tauber	$26	Currency swaps, forwards, and options	Fraud, breach of fiduciary duty, violations of state bucketing and gambling laws, and transactions in dispute were illegal off-exchange futures and options under the CEA	Salomon Brothers	In a ruling later affirmed by the Fourth Circuit Court, the U.S. District Court for the Eastern District of Virginia rejected all of Tauber's state-based defenses and counterclaims. In addition, the court concluded that the disputed transactions were exempt from the CEA and thereby rejected all of the counterclaims asserting that the dealer had violated the CEA.
10	Gibson Greetings, Inc.	$21	Interest rate swaps and options	Fraudulent concealment, breach of fiduciary duty, reckless and negligent misrepresentation, and violations of the CEA's general fraud section (4b) and fraud by a commodidites trading advisor (4o)	Bankers Trust	The parties settled, with Bankers Trust forgiving $14 million of the $21 million owed to it by Gibson Greetings.
11	Sinochem	$20	Interest rate swaps	Transaction conducted with unauthorized end-user personnel	Lehman Brothers	The parties settled for an undisclosed amount.

No.	Entity or individual reporting losses	Loss amount (millions)[a]	Specific type of derivative product	Relevant lawsuit claims, defenses, or counterclaims	Dealer	Outcome of lawsuit
12	PT Adimitra Rayapratama	$16	Interest rate swaps	Breach of fiduciary duty, professional negligence, negligent misrepresentation, violation of the CEA commodities trading advisor fraud section (4o), and violation of the Racketeer Influenced and Corrupt Organizations Act (RICO)	Bankers Trust	The U.S. District Court for the Southern District of New York dismissed the federal commodities and RICO claims because they were precluded by the parties' contractual choice of the law of England. The court also dismissed the common law claims that remained because the dismissal of the federal law claims removed its jurisdiction over those claims. The parties subsequently settled for an undisclosed amount.
13	Equity Group Holdings	$11	Interest rate (bond) options	Negligent misrepresentation and breach of fiduciary duty	Bankers Trust	The parties settled for an undisclosed amount.

[a] The loss amounts reported may include realized losses, unrealized losses, losses arising in part from products or activities other than OTC derivatives, or the amount of the loss may be in dispute.
Sources: Court documents, journal articles, press accounts, and interviews with dealer officials.

Annex 1 through 6 to *Supervisory Information Framework for Derivatives and Trading Activities* (Joint Report by the Basle Committee on Banking Supervision and the Technical Committee of the "IOSCO")

ANNEX 1: FRAMEWORK FOR SUPERVISORY INFORMATION ON DERIVATIVES AND TRADING ACTIVITIES

Use	*Description*
IX Credit Risk (OTC Contracts)	Risk of loss (aggregated across all activities) due to counterparty default. To the extent possible, credit risk from on- and off-balance-sheet instruments should be considered together.
(A) Current Credit Exposure	Positive Replacement Cost: 1. Netted to reflect legally enforceable bilateral netting agreements (also consider average and range of values over reporting period). 2. Gross by type—interest rate, foreign exchange, equity, precious metals and other commodities.
(B) Potential Credit Exposure Data allowing independent supervisory assessment of exposure	Gross Notionals 1. By type—interest rate, foreign exchange, equity, precious metals and other commodities. 2. Maturity—one year or less, over one year through five years, over five years.
Data reflecting institution's assessment using internal models	Internally-generated estimates of potential credit risk calculated by counterparty and summed. Utilize model specifications and parameters that are either designated by the supervisor, or currently employed by the individual institutions in the risk management process.

Source: Supervisory information framework for derivatives and trading activities (Joint report by the Basle Committee on Banking Supervision and the technical committee of the "IOSCO").

177

(C) Credit Enhancements	
Collateral—How much of credit exposure is collateralized?	Market value of collateral held against netted current and potential exposure.
Collateral Agreements—How much of potential exposure is subject to collateral agreements?	Notional amount and market value of contracts with agreements to provide additional collateral, should credit exposure increase.
(D) Concentration of Credit	Number of counterparties with current and potential credit exposures greater than a specified minimum level of the reporter's capital. Total exposure to these counterparts (positive net replacement cost and potential credit exposure). Counterparty credit exposure is better evaluated by taking into consideration both cash-instrument and off-balance-sheet relationships. Supervisors may also wish to obtain information on an institution's aggregate exposures to various exchanges and on their exposures to certain types of collateral.
(E) Counterparty Credit Quality	Total positive net replacement cost and potential credit exposure by counterparty credit quality (by Basle Capital Accord risk-weights, by rating agency grades, or by internal ratings).
	Information on past-due status and actual credit losses, by major counterparties and in the aggregate.
X Liquidity Risk	Market liquidity risk—risk that position cannot be liquidated or hedged.
	Funding risk—insufficient cash-flow or liquid assets to meet cash-flow require-ments. (In addition to information below, information about the notional amounts and expected cash flows of derivatives according to specified time intervals.)

(A) Identify potential market liquidity exposures	Notional amounts and market values for exchange-traded and OTC derivatives by market and product type:
	
	— OTC
	
	   ■ Interest Rate—forwards, swaps, amortising swaps, option products
	   ■ Foreign Exchange—forwards, swaps, option products
	   ■ Equities
	   ■ Commodities and other
	
	— Exchange-Traded Futures and Options
	
	   ■ Interest rate
	   ■ Foreign exchange
	   ■ Equity
	   ■ Commodity and other
	
	Notional amounts and expected cash in and outflows by maturities.

(B) Identify OTC contracts with triggering provisions.	Notionals and positive and negative market value of contracts with triggering provisions (this information combined gives a picture of the net flows, in and out, resulting from contracts with triggers): — that require the institution to liquidate or post collateral in the wake of adverse events affecting it; — that the institution can require its counterparty to liquidate or post collateral in the wake of adverse events affecting that counterparty.
(C) Market activity	Notional amounts and gross positive and gross negative market value of derivatives by risk category and contract type. This data could be aggregated across institutions to provide information on total market size.
XI Market Risk of Trading and Derivatives Activities	Risk of loss from adverse changes in market prices—data will need to be collected separately for trading and non-trading portfolios. Data could be collected by broad risk category (i.e., interest rate, foreign exchange, equities, commodities, etc.). Market risk best assessed from a portfolio context.

Position data allowing independent supervisory assessment using the standardized approach	For example: — Net open positions (longs minus shorts) by risk category (interest rate, foreign exchange, equities, commodities). — For equity contracts, net open positions by individual issues. — For interest rate and commodities contracts, net open positions by maturities. Duration information on interest rate positions. — Options could be included on a delta-equivalent basis. Other data for alternative supervisory models or screening criteria.
Data on institution's internal assessment of market risk (internal models approach)	Internally generated estimate of market risk through a value-at-risk (VaR) methodology, earnings-at-risk, duration or gap analysis, or some other methodology. For information on VaR, can use model specifications and parameters that are either designated by supervisors or currently employed by individual institutions in the risk management process. These include: 1. Position sensitivities 2. Market risk factor volatilities 3. Market risk factor correlations 4. Historical sample period and holding period 5. Confidence interval
	Information on the average and range of VaR estimates over the reporting period more informative than point in time estimates. Internal model validation information: 1. Comparisons of estimated risk vs. actual results—back-testing 2. Major assumptions underlying models

Results of stress tests. The stress test could be specified by supervisors, the institution itself, or by a combination of both.	Analysis of likelihood of "worst case" scenarios, preferably on an institution-wide basis. Identification of major assumptions. Qualitative analysis of actions management might take under particular scenarios.
XII Earnings	
(A) Trading purposes	Revenues from trading activities (derivatives and cash instruments) by risk type (interest rate, foreign exchange, equities, commodities and other) or by major trading desks (bonds, swaps, FX, equities, etc.).
(B) Purposes other than trading	Impact on net income: net increase (decrease) in interest income, net increase (decrease) in interest expense and other (non-interest allocations).
(C) Identify unrealized or deferred losses	Notional amounts, market values and unrealized losses of derivatives held on an accrual basis. Amount of realized losses on derivatives that have been deferred. Could be collected either by instrument or in total.
(D) Derivatives valuation reserves and actual credit losses	Amount of valuation reserves or provisions and actual credit losses, and their earnings impact.

ANNEX 2: DERIVATIVES DATA ELEMENTS AND THEIR USES

Element	*Use*
1. Gross or Effective Notionals:	
OTC by Contract Type	Credit and Liquidity Risks
Exchange-Traded by Contract Type	Credit and Liquidity Risks
Position (Long and Short)	Market Risk
2. Positive Net Replacement Cost	Credit Risk
3. Gross Positive Market Value by Broad Risk Category	Market Activity, Credit Risk and Liquidity Risk
4. Gross Negative Market Value by Broad Risk Category	Market Activity and Liquidity Risk
5. Collateral	Credit Risk (Current and Potential Credit Exposure)
6. Contracts with Collateral Agreements	Potential Credit Exposure and Liquidity Risk
7. Counterparty Exposures Identified Risk Weight or Investment Rating (Positive Net Replacement Cost and Potential Credit Exposure)	Credit Risk (Counterparty Credit by Quality)
8. Notional Amounts for Broad Risk Categories of Derivatives by Maturities	Potential Credit Exposure, Market Risk, Liquidity Risk
9. Internal Estimate of Potential Credit Exposure	Credit Risk (Potential Exposure)
10. Counterparties with Significant Netted Credit Exposure	Concentration of Credit Risk
11. Contracts with Trigging Provisions	Liquidity Risk
12. Market Value of Contracts Held for Other than Trading	Earnings, Credit Risk
13. Internal "Value-at-Risk" Estimates by Broad Risk Categories (Including Interest Rates, Foreign Exchange Rates, Commodity and Equity Prices)	Market Risk
14. Position Data (Longs and Shorts) for Debt Securities, Equities, Foreign Exchange and Commodities	Market Risk

15. Trading Revenues (Cash and Derivative Instruments) by Risk Type (Includes Interest Rate, Foreign Exchange, Equity, Commodity, etc.)	Earnings
16. Impact on Net Income (Net Interest Income, Net Interest Expense and Other Non-interest Allocations) of Derivatives Held for Purposes Other Than Trading	Earnings
17. Unrealized and Deferred Losses	Earnings
18. Valuation Reserves and Credit Losses	Earnings, Credit Risk

ANNEX 3: COMMON MINIMUM INFORMATION FRAMEWORK

TABLE 1   Notional Amounts by Underlying Exposures

Notional Amounts[1]	Interest Rate Contracts	Foreign Exchange and Gold Contracts[2]	Precious Metals (Other Than Gold) Contracts	Other Commodity Contracts	Equity-Linked Contracts
OTC contracts					
Forwards					
Swaps					
Purchased options					
Written options					
Exchange-traded contracts					
Futures—long positions					
Futures—short positions					
Purchased options					
Written options					
Total contracts held for trading[3]					
Total contracts held for other than trading					

[1] While included in this table's aggregate information, supervisors may wish to obtain separate information on certain categories of higher risk derivative instruments or summary information on new forms of derivatives (e.g., credit derivatives), as appropriate.
[2] This does not include spot foreign exchange, which may be assessed as a separate item. While included in the aggregate information in this column, for securities firms, information on the notional amounts of gold contracts should be evaluated separately.
[3] For purposes of these totals, all derivative instruments of securities firms will be considered to be in the "contracts held for trading" category.

TABLE 2   OTC Notional Amounts, Market Values and Potential Credit Exposure

Total Notionals, Market Values and Potential Credit Exposure[1]	Interest Rate Contracts	Foreign Exchange and Gold Contracts[2]	Precious Metals (Other Than Gold) Contracts	Other Commodity Contracts	Equity-Linked Contracts
Total notional amounts[3]					
Contracts held for trading purposes[4]					
(a) Gross positive market value					
(b) Gross negative market value					
Contracts held for other than trading					
(a) Gross positive market value					
(b) Gross negative market value					
Potential credit exposure[5]					

[1] While included in this table's aggregate information, supervisors may wish to obtain separate information on certain categories of higher risk derivative instruments, as appropriate.

[2] This does not include spot foreign exchange, which may be assessed as a separate item. While included in the aggregate information in this column, for securities firms, information on the notional amounts, market value and potential future exposure of gold contracts should be evaluated separately.

[3] The "total notional amounts" reflected on this line are the sum of the notional amounts of the OTC contracts summarized in Table 1.

[4] For purposes of these totals, all derivative instruments of securities firms will be considered to be in the "contracts held for trading" category.

[5] For banks, information on potential credit exposure should be in accordance with the Basle Capital Accord. Securities firms should use approaches acceptable to their regulator in estimating these amounts.

TABLE 3
OTC Derivative Contracts' Notional Amounts by Time Intervals

OTC Contracts[1]	One year or less	Over One Year through Five Years	Over Five Years
(a) Interest rate contracts			
Purchased options			
(b) Foreign exchange and gold contracts[2]			
Purchased options			
(c) Precious metals (other than gold) contracts			
Purchased options			
(d) Other commodity contracts			
Purchased options			
(e) Equity-linked contracts			
Purchased options			

[1] While included in this table's aggregate information, supervisors may wish to obtain separate information on certain categories of higher risk derivative instruments, as appropriate.

[2] This does not include spot foreign exchange, which may be assessed as a separate item. While included in the aggregate information in this column, for securities firms, information on the notional amounts (by time intervals) of gold contracts should be evaluated separately.

Note: The information in this table is based on the remaining maturity of the derivative instrument. Supervisors may also want to evaluate information about options (by the broad risk categories noted above) based on the maturity of the underlying.

TABLE 4
Information on Credit Quality of OTC Derivative Contracts

Counterparty Credit Quality*	Exposure before Collateral and Guarantees			Credit Equivalent Amount after Collateral and Guarantees
	Gross Positive Market Value	Current Credit Exposure	Potential Credit Exposure	
1				
2				
3				
Total				

Credit Quality*	Collateral	Guarantees
1		
2		
3		

---

*Credit quality categories would be defined as follows
[1] For banks, category 1 identifies counterparties given a 0% risk weight under the Basle Capital Accord. For securities firms, category 1 identifies counterparties rated AA and above.
[2] For banks, category 2 identifies counterparties given a 20% risk weight under the Basle Capital Accord. For securities firms, category 2 identifies counterparties rated BBB and above.
[3] For banks, category 3 identifies counterparties given a 50% risk weight under the Basle Capital Accord. For securities firms, category 3 identifies counterparties rated below BBB.
Note: When basing the above categories on ratings, an institution's equivalent internal credit grade ranking may be used when investment ratings are not available. Moreover, in addition to using the credit quality categories based on Basle Accord risk weights, bank supervisors may wish to assess the above information by credit ratings assigned by external ratings agencies or by an institution's internal credit grade rankings.

TABLE 5

Information about Past-Due OTC Derivatives and Credit Losses[1]

Book value of derivatives past-due 30–89 days
Book value of derivatives past-due 90 days or more[2]
Gross positive market value of derivatives past due 30–89 days
Gross positive market value of derivatives past-due 90 days or more[2]
Credit losses on derivative instruments during the period

---

[1] Certain countries may apply different maturity breakdowns when assessing past-due derivatives.

Also, supervisors may wish to consider information on derivatives that have been restructured due to deterioration in counterparty credit quality or past-due status, together with information on collateral and guarantees supporting these exposures.

While included in this table's aggregate information, supervisors may wish to obtain separate information on certain categories of higher risk derivative instruments, as appropriate.

[2] Information about derivatives that are past-due 90 days or more should also include in formation about derivatives that, while not technically past-due, are with counterparties that are not expected to pay the full amounts owed to the institution under the derivative contracts.

ANNEX 4: EXAMPLES OF MARKET RISK INFORMATION UNDER AN INTERNAL MODELS APPROACH[21]

1. EXAMPLES OF VALUE-AT-RISK (VaR) INFORMATION

The channels for collecting summary information, such as the type of information shown below, should be flexible, as discussed in the catalogue section. The risk management reports of well-managed institutions provide timely and accurate information on the main sources of risk within each broad category (e.g., showing the interest rate risk which arises from positions in specific types of securities and derivatives). Moreover, comprehensive risk management reports (consistent with information that institutions use to manage their risks) usually can provide more complete and relevant market risk information than fixed-format regulatory reports.

This annex presents examples of VaR information that are routinely developed by internationally active banks and securities firms under an internal models approach.

(a)   Broad VaR data for the trading and derivatives activities of the entire bank or securities firm—at the reporting date, and the average, minimum, and maximum for the period.

(b)   VaR information for each category below—at the reporting date, and the average, minimum, and maximum for the period. Further VaR information should be provided by risk factors or business lines or other relevant subcategories based on the risk management structure of the banks or securities firms.

- Interest Rate (1)
- Equity (1)
- Foreign Exchange
- Commodities
- Correlated Risk Factors

(1) Under the Basle Committee's September 1997 amendment to the Capital Accord, these elements could be further refined to present information on specific risk associated with these risk categories when an institution is able to model specific risk separately.

---

[21] For banks: Under the Basle Committee's guidance on market risk capital requirements (January 1996 and September 1997 amendments to the Basle Capital Accord).

2. BACKGROUND INFORMATION ON PARAMETERS FOR ESTIMATING VaR

The model review process undertaken by supervisors will serve as the main source of qualitative and quantitative information about the assumptions underlying the institution's internal models and related VaR estimates. This type of information is primarily needed at the time of model validation or on-site examination, or when significant changes in modeling techniques occur. The quantitative information must be assessed in the context of qualitative information about the institution's risk management and internal control process.

1. Confidence interval.[22]
2. Holding period.[23]
3. Type of risk measurement model used (e.g., variance/covariance, historical simulation, Monte-Carlo simulation).
4. The risk factors and the method of aggregation across risk factor categories (e.g., ranging from simple-sum aggregation to full recognition of correlations).
5. Method for calculating the n-day price shock (e.g., VaR based on one-day price moves scaled up to n-days or full n-day price moves).
6. Calendar dates that the historical observation period covers.
7. For interest rate risk, the number of risk factors (maturity buckets) used and the method of capturing spread risk.
8. For equity risk, the method of modeling equity risk (e.g., broad market indices, beta equivalents, or a separate risk factor for each equity).
9. The treatment of options:
   - Full n-day price shock or 1 day VaR scaled up by the square root of n.

---

[22] For internationally active banks, the confidence interval is 99 percent.
[23] For internationally active banks, the holding period is 10 days.

- Method of determining change in price of underlying (e.g., Monte Carlo simulation or variance/covariance approach).
- Method of revaluation (e.g., full revaluation model or Taylor Series expansion).
- Method of measuring volatility risk and how aggregated with other risk factors.

3. EXAMPLE OF STRESS TESTING INFORMATION

- Basic information on scenarios applied and their impact on earnings.

4. EXAMPLE OF BACKTESTING INFORMATION

- Supervisors may require prompt reporting about significant exceptions from backtesting programmes.
- Chart of daily VaR or daily trading income compared to daily VaR.
- Number of times VaR was exceeded by actual results (based on static or dynamic backtesting).

ANNEX 5: EXAMPLES OF MARKET RISK INFORMATION UNDER A STANDARDISED APPROACH

Describe the Type of Aggregation across the Bank or Securities Firm

Interest Rate Position	Zone 1 (1)		Zone 2 (1)		Zone 3 (1)	
General Risk	Long Positions	Short Positions	Long Positions	Short Positions	Long Positions	Short Positions
Major currency 1						
Major currency 2						
...						
Major currency N						
Total						

Please describe the methodology (maturity method or duration method). If different methods are used for different entities of the group, or for different portfolios, please provide separate tables.

Interest Rate Position (2)	Government	Qualifying Elements	Standard 8%	Others
Specific Risk				

Equity Positions	Net Long Positions	Net Short Positions
Major market 1		
Major market 2		
...		
Major market N		
Total		

Foreign Exchange Positions	Net Long Positions	Net Short Positions
Currency 1		
Currency 2		
Currency 3		
...		
Total Net Position		
Gold		

Commodities Positions	Long Positions	Short Positions
Precious metals (excluding Gold)		
Other Commodities		

---

(1) These positions should be broken down by their residual maturity or their sensitivity, according to relevant time horizons (e.g., for banks, under the Basle Committee capital rules, short-term, medium-term, or long-term time horizons may be used, with the possibility of finer time breakdowns aligned with the structure of the yield curve).

(2) Sum of net long and net short positions.

EXAMPLE OF THE ESTIMATION OF MARKET RISK CAPITAL ALLOCATION ACCORDING TO A STANDARDISED APPROACH

- For banks, this information relates to the capital charge under the market risk amendment to the Basle Capital Accord.
- For securities firms, this information may refer to the internally allocated capital or to the regulatory capital charge, when applicable.

Risk Category	Capital Allocation
INTEREST RATE	
General market risk	
—Net position (parallel shift)	
—Horizontal disallowance (curvature)	
—Vertical disallowance (basis)	
—Options (1)	
Specific risk	
EQUITY	
General market risk	
Specific risk	
Options	
FOREIGN EXCHANGE	
Options	
COMMODITIES	
TOTAL (Standardised Approach)	

(1) Additional charge for Gamma and Vega risk under Delta-Plus approach of charge for carved-out options and underlying exposure—under simplified and scenario approach.

ANNEX 6: DEFINITIONS FOR ELEMENTS OF THE COMMON MINIMUM INFORMATION FRAMEWORK

I. INTRODUCTION

This set of definitions refers to items identified in the common minimum information framework for derivative instruments. These definitions are intended to assist supervisors when analysing information about institutions' derivatives activities by improving the consistency and comparability of this information. The information presented below is intended as supplemental guidance to the notes in Tables 1–5 of the common minimum information framework *in annex 3.*

II. GENERAL CONCEPTS

(a) Broad Risk Categories (Tables 1–3)

For supervisory analysis purposes, five broad risk categories for derivative contracts are used in the common minimum information framework. Derivative contracts with multiple risk characteristics should be categorised based on the predominant risk characteristics at the origination of the contract. These five broad risk categories are summarised below.

   1. *Interest rate contracts:* Interest rate contracts are contracts related to an interest-bearing financial instrument or whose cash flows are determined by referencing interest rates or another interest rate contract (e.g., an option on a futures contract to purchase a domestic government bond). These contracts are generally used to adjust the institution's interest rate exposure or, if the institution is an intermediary, the interest rate exposure of others. Interest rate contracts include single currency interest rate swaps, basis swaps, forward rate agreements, futures contracts committing the institution to purchase or sell financial instruments with the predominant risk characteristic being interest rate risk, and interest rate options, including caps, floors, collars and corridors.

   Excluded are contracts involving the exchange of one or more foreign currencies (e.g., cross-currency swaps and currency options) and other contracts whose predominant risk characteristic is foreign exchange risk, which should be evaluated as foreign exchange contracts.

Excluded are commitments to purchase and sell when-issued securities from interest rate contracts. Supervisors may wish to evaluate these separately.

2. *Foreign exchange contracts:* Foreign exchange contracts are contracts to purchase or to sell foreign currencies or contracts whose cash flows are determined by reference to foreign currencies. Foreign currency contracts include forward foreign exchange, currency futures, currency options, currency warrants and currency swaps. Such contracts are usually used to adjust an institution's foreign currency exposure or, if the institution is an intermediary, the foreign exchange exposure of others. Spot foreign exchange contracts can be excluded from this definition, as they are not derivative instruments. All amounts reflected as foreign exchange contracts should be translated into the institution's base (or functional) currency.

For the purpose of supervisory analysis, only one side of a foreign currency transaction should be reported. In those transactions where foreign currencies are bought or sold against an institution's base currency, include only that side of the transaction which involves the foreign currency. For example, if a US institution with a base currency of US dollars enters into a futures contract in which it purchases US dollars against Deutsche Marks, then the amount of Deutsche Marks sold would be reflected as a foreign exchange contract (in US dollar equivalent values). Consistent with this approach, in cross-currency transactions, which involve the purchase and sale of two foreign currencies, only the purchase side should be reflected in the information about foreign exchange contracts.

For purposes of this analysis, bank supervisors should evaluate gold contracts together with foreign exchange contracts. Supervisors of banks and securities firms may also wish to evaluate information about gold contracts separately.

3. *Precious metals (other than gold) contracts:* All contracts that have a return, or portion of their return, linked to the price of silver, platinum or palladium contracts, or to an index of precious metals other than gold, should be reflected in this broad risk category.

4. *Other commodity contracts:* Other commodity contracts are contracts that have a return, or a portion of their return, linked to the price of or to an index of a commodity such as petroleum, lumber, agricultural products, or to non-ferrous metals such as copper or zinc. Other commodity contracts also include any other contracts that are not appropriately categorised as interest rate, foreign exchange and gold, other precious metals or equity derivative contracts.

5. *Equity-linked contracts:* Equity-linked derivative contracts are contracts that have a return, or a portion of their return, linked to the price of a particular equity or to an index of equity prices, such as the Standard and Poor's 500 or the Nikkei.

(b) Purposes for Holding Derivative Instruments (Tables 1–2)

1. *Contracts held for trading purposes:* Contracts held for trading purposes include those used in dealing and other trading activities accounted for at market value (or at lower of cost or market value) with gains and losses recognised in earnings. Derivative instruments used to hedge trading activities should also be reflected as derivatives held for trading purposes.

Derivative trading activities include (a) regularly dealing in interest rate contracts, foreign exchange contracts, equity derivative contracts and other off-balance-sheet commodity contracts; (b) acquiring or taking positions in such items principally for the purpose of selling in the near term or otherwise with the intent to resell (or repurchase) in order to profit from short-term price movements; or (c) acquiring or taking positions in such items as an accommodation to customers.

2. *Contracts held for purposes other than trading:* Derivative contracts that are held for purposes other than trading include (a) off-balance-sheet contracts used to hedge debt and equity securities not in the institution's trading accounts; (b) foreign exchange contracts that are designated as, and are effective as, economic hedges of items not in trading accounts; and (c) other off-balance-sheet contracts used to hedge other assets or liabilities not held for trading purposes. Included in this information is the notional amount or par value of contracts such as swap contracts intended to hedge interest rate risk on commercial loans that are accounted for on a historical cost basis.

(c) Notional Amounts (Tables 1–3)

1. *General concepts:* Notional amounts reflect the gross par value (e.g., for futures, forwards and option contracts) or the notional amount (e.g., for forward rate agreements and swaps), as appropriate, for all off-balance-sheet contracts. These contracts should be evaluated under the broad risk categories summarised in II.(a). Furthermore, these notional amounts should be stated in local currency.

For purposes of the common minimum information framework, the notional amount or par value for an off-balance-sheet derivative contract with a multiplier component is the contract's *effective* notional amount or par value. For example, a swap contract with a stated notional amount of $1,000,000 whose terms call for quarterly settlement of the difference between 5% and LIBOR multiplied by 10 has an effective notional amount of $10,000,000.

2. *Special considerations for gold contracts, precious metals (other than gold) contracts and other commodity contracts:* The contract amount for commodity and other contracts should be the quantity, i.e., number of units, of the commodity or product contracted for purchase or sale multiplied by the contract price of a unit.

The notional amount for a commodity contract with multiple exchanges of principal is the contractual amount multiplied by the number of remaining payments (or exchanges of principal) in the contract.

3. *Special considerations for equity-linked contracts:* The contract amount for equity derivative contracts is the quantity, i.e., number of units, of the equity instrument or equity index contracted for purchase or sale multiplied by the contract price of a unit.

4. *Notional amounts of OTC derivatives by time intervals (Table 3):* Table 3 summarises the notional amounts or par value of OTC off-balance-sheet contracts included in Tables 1 and 2 that are subject to credit risk. (For banks, these OTC contracts are subject to risk-based capital requirements.) Such contracts include swaps, forwards and OTC purchased options. The notional amounts and par values should be presented in the column corresponding to the contract's remaining term to maturity from the evaluation date. For supervisory analysis purposes, the remaining maturities are (1) one year or less; (2) over one year through five years; and

(3) over five years. Supervisors may also want to evaluate information about purchased options based on the maturity of the underlying.

This information on notional amounts should not reflect the notional amount for single currency interest rate swaps in which payments are made based upon two floating rate indices, so-called floating/floating or basis swaps; foreign exchange contracts with an original maturity of fourteen days or less; and futures contracts.

The notional amount for an amortising off-balance-sheet derivative contract is the contract's current (or, if appropriate, effective) notional amount. This notional amount should be reflected in the column corresponding to the contract's remaining term to final maturity.

(d) Gross Positive and Negative Market Values (Tables 2, 3 and 5 Present Information on Gross Positive Market Values; Table 2 Presents Information on Gross Negative Market Values)

1. The market value of an off-balance-sheet derivative contract is the amount at which a contract could be exchanged in a current transaction between willing parties, other than in a forced or liquidation sale. If a quoted market price is available for a contract, the market value for that contract is the product of the number of trading units of the contract multiplied by that market price. If a quoted market price is not available, the institution's best estimate of market value could be used, based on the quoted market price of a similar contract or on valuation techniques such as discounted cash flows. Market values should be reflected in the local currency of the institution.

2. Gross positive market values represent the loss that an institution would incur in the event of a counterparty default, as measured by the cost of replacing the contract at current market rates or prices. (This measure does not reflect reductions in credit exposure that would occur under legally enforceable netting arrangements.)

(e) Current Credit Exposure (Table 4)

1. Current credit exposure (sometimes referred to as the replacement cost) is the market value of a contract when that value is positive. Current credit exposure amounts for OTC off-balance-sheet derivative contracts reflect consideration of the effects of applicable legally enforceable bilateral netting agreements.

2. For banks, current credit exposure amounts should be consistent with the risk-based capital standards. The current credit exposure is zero when the market value is negative or zero. Current credit exposure should be derived as follows: determine whether a legally enforceable bilateral netting agreement is in place between the institution and a counterparty. If such an agreement is in place, the market values of all applicable contracts with that counterparty that are included in the netting agreement are netted to a single amount. Next, for all other contracts covered by the risk-based capital standards that have positive market values, the total of the positive market values is determined. Then, current credit exposure is the sum of (i) the net positive market values of applicable contracts subject to legally enforceable bilateral netting agreements and (ii) the total positive market values of all other contracts covered by the risk-based capital standards.

The definition of a legally enforceable bilateral netting agreement for purposes of this item is the same as that set forth in the risk-based capital rules.

(f) Information on Credit Quality of OTC Derivative Contracts (Table 4)

1. Gross positive market value and current credit exposure have been defined in II.(d) and II.(e) above.

2. Potential credit exposure is the exposure of the derivative contract that may be realised over its remaining life due to movements in the rates or prices underlying the contract.

For banks, under the Basle Capital Accord, potential credit exposure is reflected through a so-called "add-on", which is calculated by multiplying the contract's gross or effective notional value by a conversion factor based on the price volatility of the underlying contract. There are separate factors for interest rate contracts, foreign exchange and gold contracts, precious metals (other than gold) contracts, other commodities contracts and equity-linked contracts—distinguishing between the remaining maturity of the contract (i.e., one year or less, over one year to five years and more than five years). The add-ons may also take account of the effects of legally valid netting agreements. For banks, information on potential credit exposure should be consistent with bank supervisory guidelines, including risk-based capital standards.

Securities firms should use approaches acceptable to their regulators in estimating potential credit exposure.

3. For banks, information on the manner in which collateral and guarantees reduce current and potential credit exposure should be consistent with the Basle Capital Accord. For securities firms, information on the effects of collateral and guarantees should reflect approaches that are acceptable to their regulators.

(g) Information about Past-Due Derivatives (Table 5)

1. The "book value" of past-due derivatives is the amounts, if any, that are recorded as assets by the institution in its balance sheet. These amounts may include amounts accrued as receivable for interest rate swaps, the unamortised amount of the premium paid for an interest rate cap or floor, or the market value of a derivative contract in a gain position that has been recorded as an asset (e.g., in a trading account) on the balance sheet.

2. The "gross positive market value" of past-due derivatives is consistent with the definition of "gross positive market value" presented above (II.(d)). These gross positive market values should be evaluated regardless of whether they have been recorded as assets on the balance sheet. This information should not include the market value of derivative instruments with negative market values.

3. Credit losses include declines in positive market values for derivatives that are associated with deteriorating counterparty credit quality, when the mark to market values of these derivatives have been recorded on the balance sheet. Credit losses may also include writeoffs of the book value of derivatives—taking these writeoffs against provisions (allowances) for credit losses.

III. DEFINITIONS OF SPECIFIC TYPES OF DERIVATIVES

(a) Futures Contracts

Futures contracts represent agreements for delayed delivery of financial instruments or commodities in which the buyer agrees to purchase and the seller agrees to deliver, at a specified future date, a specified instrument at a specified price or yield. Futures contracts are standardised and are traded on organised exchanges where the exchange or a clearing house acts as the counterparty to each contract.

(b) Forward Contracts

Forward contracts represent agreements for delayed delivery of financial instruments or commodities in which the buyer agrees to purchase and the seller agrees to deliver, at a specified future date, a specified instrument or commodity at a specified price or yield. Forward contracts are not traded on organised exchanges and their contractual terms are not standardised.

(c) Option Contracts

1. Option contracts convey either the right or the obligation, depending upon whether the institution is the purchaser or the writer, respectively, to buy or sell a financial instrument or commodity at a specified price on or before a specified future date. Some options are traded on organised exchanges. Also, options can be written to meet the specialised needs of the counterparty to the transaction. These customised option contracts are known as over-the-counter (OTC) options. Thus, over-the-counter option contracts include all option contracts not traded on an organised exchange.

2. The buyer of an option contract has, for compensation (such as a fee or premium), acquired the right (or option) to sell to, or purchase from, another party some financial instrument or commodity at a stated price on or before a specified future date. The seller of the contract has, for such compensation, become obligated to purchase or sell the financial instrument or commodity at the option of the buyer of the contract. A put option contract obligates the seller of the contract to purchase some financial instrument or commodity at the option of the buyer of the contract. A call option contract obligates the seller of the contract to sell some financial instrument or commodity at the option of the buyer of the contract.

3. In addition, swaptions, i.e., OTC options to enter into a swap contract, and OTC contracts known as caps, floors, collars and corridors, should be reflected as options for supervisory analysis purposes.

4. Generally, options such as a call feature that are embedded in loans, securities and other on-balance-sheet assets and commitments to lend are not included in the supervisory analysis reflected in Tables 1–5. Supervisors may wish to evaluate these embedded options separately in certain situations.

5. *Purchased options:* When assessing information on purchased options in Table 1, this information should reflect the aggregate notional or par value of the financial instruments or commodities which the institution has, for a fee or premium, purchased the right to either purchase or sell under exchange-traded or OTC option contracts that are outstanding as of the evaluation date. Also, include in OTC purchased options an aggregate notional amount for purchased caps, floors and swaptions and for the purchased portion of collars and corridors.

6. *Written options:* When evaluating information on written options for Table 1, this information should reflect the aggregate notional or par value of the financial instruments or commodities that the institution has, for compensation (such as a fee or premium), obligated itself to either purchase or sell under exchange-traded or OTC option contracts that are outstanding as of the evaluation date. Also reflect as written options the aggregate notional amount for written caps, floors and swaptions and for the written portion of collars and corridors.

(d) Swaps

Swaps are OTC transactions in which two parties agree to exchange payment streams based on a specified notional amount for a specified period. Forward starting swap contracts should be evaluated as swaps. The notional amount of a swap is the underlying principal amount upon which the exchange of interest, foreign exchange or other income or expense is based. The notional amount for a swap contract with a multiplier component is the contract's effective notional amount. In those cases where the institution is acting as an intermediary, both sides of the transaction should be reflected in the information in Table 1.

(e) Credit Derivatives

1. For purposes of the common minimum framework, credit derivatives are arrangements that allow one party (the "beneficiary") to transfer the credit risk of a "reference asset," which it may or may not actually own, to another party (the "guarantor"). These instruments allow the guarantor to assume the credit risk associated with a reference asset without directly purchasing it.

2. Under some credit derivative arrangements, the beneficiary may pay the total return on a reference asset, including any appreciation in the asset's price, to a guarantor in exchange for a spread over funding costs plus any depreciation in the value of the reference asset (a "total rate-of-return swap"). Alternatively, a beneficiary may pay a fee to the guarantor in exchange for a guarantee against any loss that may occur if the reference asset defaults (a "credit default swap"). Other types of on-balance-sheet instruments exist with features that are similar to the credit derivatives discussed above.

INDEX

ABSs, 33
Accountability (*see* Supervising the derivatives trading program)
Accounting risk, 50–52
Accredited investors, 41
Add-ons, 115, 200, 201
American-style options, 7, 8
Asian flu, 101
Asset-backed securities (ABSs), 33

Background check, 109
Baring's Bank, 52, 53, 141–169
Basle Committee on Banking Supervision, 113
Basle/IOSCO report, 113–120
    Annexes 1-6, 177–204
    credit risk, 114–117
    earnings risk, 119, 120
    liquidity risk, 117, 118
    market risk, 118, 119
    VAR methodology, 118, 119
Bismarck, Otto von, 136
Board of Governors of Federal Reserve Board, 133, 135
Bottom fishing, 56
Boundary risk, 52, 53
Brent market, 40

Call option, 7–9, 203
Cap, 14, 15, 203
Career risk, 61, 140
Case studies (*see* Real-life examples)
CFTC:
    clearing mechanism, 127
    constituency stroking, 138, 139
    creation, 132
    forward contracts, and, 40
    futures contracts, 32
    hybrid instruments, and, 37–39
    institutional investors, and, 41, 42
    jurisdiction, 34, 133
    leverage contract merchants, and, 137
    nonsecurity options, 33, 39
    O-T-C derivatives, and, 41
    other regulatory agencies, and, 133, 134
    oversight committees in Congress, 135
    preemption, 34
    Sumitomo Corporation, and, 63–95
    swap dealer, action against, 59
Cherrypicking, 47
Chicago Board of Trade, 25, 26, 132
Chicago Board Options Exchange, 25
China, 102
Clearing, 45
Clearinghouse, 6
Collar, 14, 15, 203
Collateral, 46
Commodity, 20–22
Commodity Exchange Act, 32, 36
Commodity Futures Trading Commission (*see* CFTC)
Commodity swap, 12, 13
Company players, 109, 110
Congress, 135, 136
Convertible debt securities (convertibles), 33
Credit and payment controls, 44–46, 124
Credit default swap, 204
Credit derivatives, 18, 21, 204
Credit risk, 46, 47, 114–117, 177, 178
Currency swap, 11–13
Customized derivatives, 2

Daily mark-to-market, 45
de Kwiatowski, Henry, 171
Department of Labor, 133
Derivatives:
    accounting treatment, 51
    customized, 2
    generic types, 2
    hedging, and, 24–29
    O-T-C (*see* Over-the-counter (O-T-C) derivatives)
    price protection, 26
    standardized, 2
    synthetics, as, 1
Disasters (*see* Real-life examples)

Earnings risk, 119, 120, 181
Earthquake bonds, 17, 18
Economic profiles:
    call option, 7
    futures contract (buyer/long position), 4
    interest rate swap, 11
    long futures hedge, 27
    put option, 9
    put option hedge (at-the-money), 28
Economic stresses, 101
Electronic trading, 123–125
    (*See also* Restructuring of derivatives
        markets)
Equity Group Holdings, 175
Equity-linked contracts, 197
Euro, 57
European-style options, 8
Exchanges, 25, 99, 100
    (*See also* Restructuring of derivatives
        markets)
Exercise price, 8
Expiration date, 8

FASB, 51, 52
Faux-merchants, 25
Federal Reserve Board, 133, 135
Federation Internationale des Bourses de
    Valeurs (FIBV), 103
Financial Accounting Standards Board
    (FASB), 51, 52
Floor, 14, 15, 203
Foreign currency swap, 11–13
Foreign exchange contracts, 196
Forrest Gump risk, 54, 55
Forward contracts, 202
    origin of, 24, 25
    regulation, 39, 40
    what are they, 19, 20
Funding risk, 117, 118, 178
Future developments (*see* Restructuring of
    derivatives markets)
Futures contracts, 3–6, 202
    economic theory, 6
    exchanges, 6
    illustrations, 5
    number of, theoretically infinite, 6
    offset election, 4
    price protection, 26
    regulation, 32

Gambling, 29
Gaming law, 34, 36, 38
General Accounting Office, 133
General Accounting Office study, 96, 97,
    171–175
Gibson Greetings, Inc., 174
Globalization, 98–100
Gold principal-indexed bonds, 16, 17
Grain market (1800s), 24, 25
Guillotine effect, 111, 112

Hamanaka, Yasuo, 62–97, 110
Hedging, 24–29
Holder, 8
Hurricane principal-indexed notes, 17
Hybrid instruments, 16–19
    CFTC, and, 37–39
    credit derivative, 18
    examples, 16, 17
    price hedge, as, 28
    regulation, 37–39
    symmetrical/asymmetrical gain and
        loss, 28

Initial margin, 44
Institutional investors, 41, 42
Interest rate contracts, 195
Interest rate swap, 10, 11, 13
International dimension, 98–104
International Organization of Securities
    Commissions (IOSCO), 103, 113
    (*See also* Basle/IOSCO report)
International Swaps and Derivatives
    Association, 104
IOSCO, 103, 113
    (*See also* Basle/IOSCO report)

J.P. Morgan, 102, 103

Leeson, Nick, 49, 110
    (*See also* Baring's Bank)
Legal climate (litigious nations), 53
Legal double-talk risk, 58, 59
Legal environment, 31–42
    exchange-traded derivatives, 32–35
    forward contracts, 39, 40

futures contracts, 32
hybrid instruments, 37
institutional investors, 41, 42
market risks, and, 31
O-T-C derivatives, 34, 35
options, 33
state laws, 32
swaps, 35, 36
[*See also* CFTC, Regulatory policy,
    Securities and Exchange Commission
    (SEC)]
Legal risk, 47, 48
Leverage contract merchants, 137
Liquidity risk, 117, 118, 178
Long, 4
Long-Term Capital Management, 42, 46

Maintenance margin, 45
Margins, 44, 45
Mark-to-market, 45
Market liquidity risk, 178
Market risk, 43, 118, 119, 179–181
Matched book, 117
Media, 139
Memoranda of understanding (MOU), 103
Minmetals, 173

National Futures Association, 57
News media, 139
Nonsecurity options, 33, 39
North Sea crude oil market, 40
Notional values, 10, 198

Office of the Comptroller of the Currency,
    133
Offset election, 4
Open outcry markets, 100, 121, 122
Operational risk, 48–50
Options, 6–9, 202, 203
    American-style, 7, 8
    call, 7–9
    European-style, 8
    evolution of, 25
    examples, 6, 8
    nonsecurity, 39
    price protection, 27
    put, 8, 9

regulations, 33
what is it, 6
Orange County bankruptcy, 19, 42, 97
Organizational oversight (*see* Supervising
    the derivatives trading program)
Other commodity contracts, 196, 197
Over-the-counter (O-T-C) derivatives, 33
    collateral, 46
    documentation, 58
    International Swaps and Derivatives
        Association, 104
    liberation from CFTC clutches, 134
    regulation, 34, 41, 42, 46
    resemblance to regulated securities, 35
    side-of-the angels risk, and, 58
    state laws, and, 134, 137
Overharvesting risk, 56, 57

Pass-through liability, 45
Pension plans, 97
Political dimension, 132–139
    Congress, 135, 136
    international considerations, 100–103
    media, 139
    regulatory agencies, 133–135
    states, 137–139
Pollyanna risk, 54
Precious metals (other than gold) contracts,
    196
Premium, 6
Pretty-face risk, 55
Proctor & Gamble, 172
PT Adimitra Rayapratama, 175
PT Dharmala Sakti Sejahtera, 173
Put option, 8, 9, 202

Ratings risk, 59, 60
RCS Editori, 171
Real-life examples:
    Baring's Bank, 52, 53, 141–169
    GAO study, 96, 97, 171–175
    Sumitomo, 62–97, 104
Regulatory agencies, 133–135
Regulatory policy:
    clearing, 45
    collateral, 46
    Congress, 135, 136
    futuristic exchanges, and, 130, 131

Regulatory policy: *(cont'd)*
    international dimensions, 103, 104
    margins, 44, 45
    mark-to-market, 45
    regulatory agencies, 133–135
    states, 137–139
    trickle-up liability, 45
    (See also CFTC, Legal environment,
        Securities and Exchange Commission
        (SEC))
Reinsurance derivatives, 28
Resignation letter, 112
Restructuring of derivatives markets, 121–131
    open outcry trading, demise of, 122, 123
    organizational chart, 129
    regulatory agencies, 130, 131
    step 1 (privatizing exchange ownership),
        125, 126
    step 2 (institutionalizing screen dealing
        mechanism, 126
    step 3 (operating self-regulatory
        program), 126
    step 4 (clearing system), 127
    step 5 (liquidating physical assets),
        127, 128
    step 6 (forming trading firm), 128
    step 7 (R–D subsidiary), 128, 129
    subsidiaries, 129, 130
Risk, 43–61
    accounting, 50–52
    boundary, 52, 53
    career, 61, 140
    credit, 46, 47, 114–117
    earnings, 119, 120
    Forrest Gump, 54, 55
    funding, 117
    legal, 47, 48
    legal double-talk, 58, 59
    liquidity, 117, 118
    market, 43, 118, 119
    operational, 48–50
    overharvesting, 56, 57
    Pollyanna, 54
    pretty-face, 55
    ratings, 59, 60
    sensitivity to (corporate policy), 60
    side-of-the-angels, 57, 58
    timing, 44–46
    valuation, 43, 44
Rogue traders, 49, 50, 61

Sales abuses, 96, 97, 171–175
    (See also Real-life examples)
Salomon Smith Barney, 60, 119
Screen dealing systems, 100, 122
Securities and Exchange Commission (SEC)
    CFTC, and, 133, 134
    institutional investors, 41
    jurisdiction reach, 33
    1997 proposal (OTC licensing system), 41
    securities-based options, 33, 39
Seita, 173
Selection process, 108, 109
Sensitivity to risk (corporate policy), 60
Short, 4
Side-of-the-angels risk, 57, 58
Sinochem, 174
SK Securities, 102, 103
Speculators, 29
Standardized derivatives, 2
State laws, 32, 34, 137–139
    (See also Gaming laws)
*Statement of Financial Accounting Standards
    No. 133: Accounting for Derivative
    Instruments and Hedging Activities*, 51
States, 137–139
Stress testing, 119
Strike price, 8
Structural changes *(see* Restructuring of
    derivatives markets)
Sumitomo Corporation, 62–97, 104
Supervising the derivatives trading
    program, 105–112
    errors, listed, 107
    step 1 (get up to speed), 107, 108
    step 2 (selection process), 108, 109
    step 3 (company players), 109, 110
    step 4 (verify/audit trading activity),
        110, 111
    step 5 (guillotine effect), 111, 112
    worst-case scenario, 105, 106
    (See also Basle/IOSCO report)
Supervisors, 49, 50
Swaps, 10–16, 203
    caps/floors/collars, 14, 15
    CFTC, and, 35, 36
    commodity, 12, 13
    contingent, 14, 16
    currency, 11–13
    economic behavior, 16
    interest rate, 10, 11, 13

regulation, 35, 36
symmetrical/asymmetrical gain and
    loss, 27
total-return security, 12, 13
Swaption, 16, 203
Symmetrical/asymmetrical gain and loss,
    27, 28
Systemic effect, 42

Tauber, Laszlo, 174
Timing risk, 44–46
Total rate-of-return swap, 204
Total-return security swap, 12, 13
Travelers Corporation, 60, 119
Treasury Department, 135
Trickle-up liability, 45
Triggering agreements, 118
Tucker, Gideon J., 136

Ultra vires, 47
Union Bank of Switzerland, 112
UNIPEC, 173

Valuation risk, 43, 44
Value-at-risk (VAR) methodology, 118, 119,
    180, 189–191

West Virginia, 172
Writer, 8

Zero sum game, 26

Philip McBride Johnson is one of the world's most highly respected derivatives attorneys with over 30 years of hands-on experience advising clients as well as running the key U.S. federal regulatory agency. He authored the legal treatise *Commodities Regulation*, which has been called "the industry's bible" in the United States, and has served the legal needs of derivatives markets around the world. Most importantly, he knows what *businesspeople* worry most about, and has captured their concerns in this book.

Head of the exchange-traded derivatives law practice at the international law firm of Skadden, Arps, Slate, Meagher & Flom, Mr. Johnson has worked closely with the world's largest futures and options exchanges, with multinational corporations, and with leading financial institutions in the derivatives arena. He literally "grew up" with the modern derivatives business from the 1960s forward, helped to develop the federal legal framework, participated in designing new derivatives products (including the world's first interest rate futures), and under President Ronald Reagan served as chairman of the U.S. Commodity Futures Trading Commission.

Mr. Johnson also helped to shape the derivatives legal practice by creating committees in the field for both the American Bar Association and the International Bar Association. Moreover, he teaches the subject at the University of Virginia School of Law and lectures frequently to both legal and business audiences. He has served on the governing boards of business trade associations and has written extensively on business aspects of the derivatives world. From those experiences, and countless hours with worried executives whose organizations were venturing into the derivatives markets for the first time, comes this book.

Mr. Johnson is referenced in *Who's Who in America* and *Who's Who in American Law*.